**Theodore Roosevelt and
the International Rivalries**

DIMITRI D. LAZO

D0167039

Theodore Roosevelt and the International Rivalries

Raymond A. Esthus / TULANE UNIVERSITY

Ginn-Blaisdell A XEROX COMPANY

WALTHAM, MASSACHUSETTS / TORONTO / LONDON

Topics in United States Diplomatic History

Consulting Editor

Norman A. Graebner, University of Virginia

Library of Congress Catalog Card Number: 71-102172.
Printed in the United States of America.

To Gloria, Jan, and Julie

Acknowledgments

Grateful acknowledgment is made to the following for permission to use copyrighted material: the President and Fellows of Harvard College and the Harvard University Press for *The Letters of Theodore Roosevelt*, edited by Elting E. Morison; Charles Scribner's Sons for *Selections from the Correspondence of Theodore Roosevelt and Henry Cabot Lodge, 1884–1918* and *The Life of Whitelaw Reid* by Royal Cortissoz; Constable and Company, Ltd., and Mrs. Sheila Moorhead for *The Letters and Friendships of Sir Cecil Spring Rice* by Stephen Gwynn; Houghton Mifflin Company and Constable and Company, Ltd., for *What Me Befell* by Jules Jusserand; Cambridge University Press for *The Holstein Papers*, edited by Norman Rich and M. H. Fisher; Robert Speller and Sons for *Three Critical Years (1904–05–06)* by Maurice Paléologue; and the University of Washington Press for *Theodore Roosevelt and Japan* by the author. For courtesies and assistance grateful appreciation is also expressed to Lady Elizabeth Arthur, the daughter of Sir Cecil Spring Rice, and to Miss Helen Mac-Lachlan, Curator of the Theodore Roosevelt Association.

R. A. E.

Contents

Introduction

Few American Presidents have played a larger role in world politics than Theodore Roosevelt. None has plunged into the maelstrom of international power rivalries with more enthusiasm and relative detachment. Woodrow Wilson, Franklin D. Roosevelt, and those who followed the second Roosevelt in the White House were drawn into the center of world affairs by circumstances that most Americans related directly to the security of the United States. Theodore Roosevelt's participation in world politics, by contrast, was not supported by any conviction on the part of the American public that the United States had an important stake in international affairs. His intervention in the international rivalries was more in the nature of a hobby. He took a leading part in composing the two great power contentions of his day, the Russo-Japanese War and the First Moroccan Crisis; yet the American public did not think the vital national interests of the United States were involved in either, at least not beyond the general interest shared by all powers in establishing and maintaining world peace.

The disinterestedness of the United States aided Roosevelt's role in world affairs in one important respect. The position of detachment which he enjoyed commanded respect and even envy in foreign capitals. At the conclusion of the Algeciras conference, Henry White, the chief United States delegate, wrote to Roosevelt that he had had an extraordinary advantage in dealing with the Moroccan dispute owing to America's policy of keeping clear of all entanglements in Europe. White reported that the venerable Italian delegate, the Marquis Visconti Venosta, had said to him again and again, "How I envy you the independence of your country which enables you to speak with such boldness and freedom to both French and Germans, as neither of them can suspect you of any hostility and both are anxious to secure your cooperation and if possible support."[1] It was the same in the Far East. After the destruction of the Russian Baltic Fleet in the Tsushima Strait in May 1905, all the major capitals of the world looked to the United States as the one power with sufficient disinterestedness to bring Russia and Japan to successful peace negotiations.

Other factors in addition to America's detachment augmented Roosevelt's influence in international affairs. One was the sheer size and potential power of the United States. Roosevelt's presidency happened to coincide with growing fears among European leaders over the possible outbreak of a world war. And however much Americans might resolve to steer clear of Old World entanglements, Europeans assumed as a matter of course that the United States would in all probability be drawn into such a war. Most leaders at London, Paris, and Berlin therefore viewed the good will and diplomatic support of the United States as well worth cultivating.

The respect and influence which the major powers accorded to Roosevelt was founded, too, on the belief that the American President could in a meaningful way actually wield the power of the United States in the world arena. This assessment, however, was based upon a fundamental misconception of Roosevelt's position. If anything comes through clearly in the indices of public opinion and Congressional sentiment of the Roosevelt period, it is that the United States was firmly committed to the concept of isolation. The detachment and disinterestedness of the United States was therefore a mixed blessing for Roosevelt, because it was a by-product of strong isolationist sentiment. This isolationism greatly limited Roosevelt's freedom of action in international affairs. The leaders of other nations never fully appreciated the extent of this limitation. The British, French, German, and Japanese Ambassadors had to constantly remind their governments that the American public would not tolerate involvement in foreign political disputes. The fact that the admonition

---

[1] White to Roosevelt, April 8, 1906, Theodore Roosevelt Papers, Library of Congress, Washington, D. C.

had to be repeated so often indicates that the message never quite got through.

Roosevelt was fully cognizant of the isolationist feelings of his countrymen, and he repeatedly cautioned foreign governments to keep his role in the power struggles absolutely secret. Fortunately for Roosevelt this was done. Though the public knew of his important work in bringing Russia and Japan to the peace table, it knew little of his diplomatic intervention in the negotiations. As for European affairs, where Roosevelt had to be even more circumspect, the public knew virtually nothing of his role in either the Anglo-German rivalry or the Franco-German rivalry.

Roosevelt was not entirely out of tune with the isolationist currents in the United States. He enjoyed intervening in foreign political disputes — he had genuine and deep concern over them — but he did not consider America's own interests in those quarrels great enough to justify incurring risks. He undertook no campaign to persuade the American public that the vital national interests of the United States were involved in the international rivalries of his day. Instead he used the instruments at hand — largely the tools of secret diplomacy — to compose the rivalries as much as he could without involving his country in responsibilities or commitments. He accepted realistically the limitations on his freedom of action and attempted to make the most of the options remaining open to him. The story of Roosevelt's role in world politics is therefore not an account of a crusader; it is rather that of a pragmatic diplomatist.

Roosevelt and the Diplomats

1

Diplomatic dispatches, instructions, and notes bored Theodore Roosevelt. To the Rough Rider the art of high diplomacy at its best meant handling affairs through face-to-face talks or through personal letters to friends and world leaders. A problem involving France would be talked over with the French Ambassador during a game of tennis. When London needed to be informed on a crucial issue, a letter would be dispatched to Cecil Spring Rice or to Arthur Lee, or one of these friends would cross the Atlantic to get the President's ideas firsthand. A conference with Secretary of State John Hay would result from Roosevelt's merely dropping by the Secretary's house during an after-supper walk. A horseback ride with Hay's successor Elihu Root would often suffice to settle some facet of the world's problems. Such personal relations with the diplomats, both American and foreign, gave Roosevelt's diplomacy a unique character.

Among the galaxy of diplomats and friends closely associated with Roosevelt in his role of world statesman, not the least in importance were his Secretaries of State, Hay and Root. Roosevelt's own energetic intervention in international affairs so dominated the scene that it created the impression that he was "his own Secretary of State," but this view does not do justice to the important parts played by Hay and Root. Roosevelt was his own Secretary of State during the six months in 1905 extending from the beginning of Hay's last and fatal illness in March until Root took active command at the Department of State in September. And this happened to be a time when diplomatic events in both Asia and Europe reached a high point, with the ending of the Russo-Japanese War and the opening stage of the Moroccan crisis. Apart from this period, however, Hay and Root successively played major roles in foreign affairs.

Roosevelt himself did not think Hay's work important, but this view was not justified. Personality differences probably account for Roosevelt's attitude in part. When he entered the White House as a young man of forty-four, Hay had already gained eminence as a diplomat and as a literary figure, and Roosevelt may have felt some jealousy. In any case the two men were poles apart in personality. Roosevelt was assertive and pugnacious; Hay was dignified and meditative. Soon after Hay's death Roosevelt told his friend Senator Henry Cabot Lodge that as a result of ill health Hay was able to do very little work of importance for two years before his death. "I had to do the big things myself," he said, "and the other things I always feared would be badly done or not done at all." [1] He later complained to John J. Leary that Hay was not a fighter, that he had lived a quiet, sheltered existence and had never been in real contact with life.[2] In 1909 he told Lodge that in the Department of State Hay's usefulness had been almost exclusively that of a fine figurehead.[3] However correct Roosevelt's assessment of Hay's personality may have been, his evaluation of Hay's role as Secretary of State was not accurate. Hay took the lead in both formulating and implementing Far Eastern policy in the years 1901–1903, and after the outbreak of the Russo-Japanese conflict in 1904 his part in the diplomacy of the war was as important as that of Roosevelt until illness struck him down in March of 1905.[4]

Root was much more to Roosevelt's liking. When Root was appointed both Roosevelt and Lodge believed the former Secretary of

---

[1] Roosevelt to Lodge, July 11, 1905, Elting E. Morison (ed.), *The Letters of Theodore Roosevelt,* 8 vols. (Cambridge, Mass.: Harvard University Press, 1951–1954), IV, 1271.

[2] John J. Leary, Jr., *Talks with T. R.* (Boston and New York: Houghton Mifflin Co., 1920), pp. 217–219.

[3] Roosevelt to Lodge, January 28, 1909, Morison, *Roosevelt Letters, VI,* 1490.

[4] Hay's work is recounted in Raymond A. Esthus, *Theodore Roosevelt and Japan* (Seattle: University of Washington Press, 1966), Chapters i–iv.

War would be an excellent Secretary of State,[5] and when Root resigned in January 1909 to enter the Senate, Roosevelt declared that he was "the greatest and ablest man who has ever filled the position of Secretary of State."[6] Roosevelt, however, overrated Root, just as he underrated Hay. Both were excellent Secretaries of State, and it would be hard to judge which surpassed the other. It is difficult to compare them, for they differed both in personality and in the way they performed their duties. Hay relied heavily upon the venerable Second Assistant Secretary of State, Alvey A. Adee, to handle the routine of the Department. Hay meanwhile gave much time to an extensive personal correspondence with diplomats at key posts abroad, writing letters which contain literary charm and incisive comments on American policy. Root's personal correspondence with American diplomats abroad was less frequent; he devoted most of his time to managing the Department at Washington. His friends and critics alike agreed that he took on his own shoulders too much of the routine work. The Third Assistant Secretary of State, Francis M. Huntington Wilson, wrote of him: "It seemed to me that his idea of Heaven would have been to stand atop a hill completely surrounded by stenographers, and attend to everything himself."[7]

Fortunately Root had a store of humor to sustain him when the details of administration weighted him down. The historical records of the Roosevelt period abound with instances of Root's wit. When Roosevelt chided him for keeping his clerks working in the Department on Sunday, Root replied:[8]

> I shall see hereafter that such work is confined strictly to the Secretary and Assistant Secretaries.
> Would it be deemed proper if we were to do work on Sunday regarding the affairs of the Far East where it is already Monday,

---

[5] Roosevelt to Lodge, July 18, 1905, Morison, *Roosevelt Letters, IV,* 1279; Lodge to Roosevelt, July 25, 1905, Henry Cabot Lodge, *Selections from the Correspondence of Theodore Roosevelt and Henry Cabot Lodge, 1884–1918,* 2 vols. (New York: Charles Scribner's Sons, 1925), *II,* 170.

[6] Roosevelt to Root, January 26, 1909, Morison, *Roosevelt Letters, VI,* 1482.

[7] Francis M. Huntington Wilson, *Memoirs of An Ex-Diplomat* (Boston: Bruce Humphries, Inc., 1945), pp. 152–153.

[8] Root to Roosevelt, March 27, 1908, Theodore Roosevelt Papers, Library of Congress, Washington, D. C.

and transfer our labors as Monday comes around and Sunday recedes, westward through the Near East and Europe?

Roosevelt chuckled and scrawled on the letter: "This is a characteristic Rootian note." Roosevelt's admiration for his Secretary was such that Root could even make the President the object of his wit, something other cabinet members did not dare. A story is told about the Panama question which, though it may be apocryphal, accurately indicates the relationship between the two men. One day when Root was Secretary of War, Roosevelt entered into a long disquisition before the cabinet attempting to justify the seizure of the canal zone. When he finished he glared around the table, finally fixing his eye on Root. "Well," he demanded belligerently, "have I answered the charges?" "You certainly have, Mr. President," said Root. "You have shown that you were accused of seduction and you have conclusively proved that you were guilty of rape." [9]

Amidst such jesting Roosevelt and Root worked together as an effective team, the elder Secretary sometimes restraining the impulsive young President. When Root took active command of the Department in September 1905, Roosevelt had completed arrangements to refer the Moroccan crisis to an international conference and the Russo-Japanese War had been settled at the Portsmouth Peace Conference, but in subsequent events Root took a significant part. He oversaw, more closely than Roosevelt, Henry White's handling of the Moroccan question at the Algeciras conference. Roosevelt took the lead in handling the problem of Japanese immigration in 1906–1907, but Root's perception of that problem was sometimes keener than Roosevelt's, and throughout the Japanese-American crises the President benefitted greatly from his Secretary's advice. Regarding the important question of America's attitude toward Japan's new position in South Manchuria in 1907–1908, Root was the key formulator of policy. Roosevelt's respect for his Secretary of State was so great that he seldom took an important step in foreign affairs without his advice and close collaboration. He once remarked of Root: "Lord, I wish you could have seen the condition in which State papers came

---

[9] Philip C. Jessup, *Elihu Root,* 2 vols. (New York: Dodd, Mead & Co., 1938), *I,* 404–405.

back to me after Root had gone over them! Sometimes I would not recognize my own child, and sometimes I was very thankful I could not." [10]

Roosevelt had little official contact with the subordinates of Hay and Root at the Department of State, though two of Root's staff were in the President's "tennis cabinet." Robert Bacon, the First Assistant Secretary of State, was — in French Ambassador Jules Jusserand's words — the "shining star" of the group that hiked and played tennis with Roosevelt.[11] He was a tall, handsome man who had rowed on the Harvard crew. Roosevelt enjoyed his friendship immensely, but the two seldom talked of foreign affairs. At the Department Bacon did not often participate in policy formulation, confining his activities largely to administrative duties and filling the role of sympathetic listener to Root's ideas.[12] William Phillips, another Harvard man, was also a member of the tennis cabinet. He had been brought to the Department from the Peking Legation in 1907 to aid the Third Assistant Secretary, Huntington Wilson, on Far Eastern Affairs, and in 1908 he became the chief of the new Far Eastern division. He was a young man who later went on to bigger duties, including the post of Ambassador to Italy during the days of Mussolini. Roosevelt often invited him to go on treks through Rock Creek Park, and the Roosevelt children found him a delightful playmate around the White House. Roosevelt was startled and amused one day to find his children and Billy Phillips noisily riding down the marble stairs of the White House in tin tubs.[13]

Other officials at the State Department did not share the fun of the White House coterie. The Second Assistant Secretary of State, Alvey A. Adee, was not suited by age or interests to adorn the tennis cabinet, though Roosevelt had frequent official contact with him during Hay's illnesses. Adee's hobbies were Shakespeare and the microscopic photography of diatomes (particles that crystalize in exquisite

---

[10] Leary, *Talks with T. R.,* p. 218.

[11] Jean Jules Jusserand, *What Me Befell: The Reminiscences of J. J. Jusserand* (Boston and New York: Houghton Mifflin Co., 1933), p. 331.

[12] Huntington Wilson, *Memoirs of An Ex-Diplomat,* pp. 153–154.

[13] William Phillips, *Ventures in Diplomacy* (Boston: Beacon Press, 1952), p. 39.

forms). Adee had served at the Department since he was appointed Third Assistant Secretary in 1882, and he was a veritable encyclopedia of precedent and of all the past business of the Department. He was very deaf and used an ear-trumpet, which he would conveniently remove when he did not wish to be bothered.

Huntington Wilson, the Third Assistant Secretary under Root, might have joined the tennis cabinet, but he felt it involved a "rather too-fawning courtship." One day when Roosevelt asked him if he liked to play tennis, he replied, "Yes, but I much prefer golf." Ambassador Lloyd Griscom, who happened to be present, whispered in his ear, "You damned fool!" [14] It probably made no difference, however, for the suave and somewhat arrogant Third Assistant Secretary would not have fitted in well with Roosevelt's circle of friends. Root eventually came to believe that Huntington Wilson was a person of the most dangerous character for diplomatic service — suspicious, egotistical and ready to take offense.[15] During the Taft administration he was named First Assistant Secretary of State, an appointment that had unfortunate effects upon relations with Japan because of his strong anti-Japanese prejudices.

Though Roosevelt's official contacts with the subordinates of Hay and Root at the State Department were limited, he had frequent dealings with American diplomats abroad and with foreign representatives in Washington. He also maintained various personal channels of communication to foreign governments. Cooperation with Britain he deemed most vital, and his links with London were more numerous than with any other capital. He carried on a personal correspondence with Joseph H. Choate and Whitelaw Reid, who served successively as Ambassadors to the Court of St. James. Hay and Root also wrote privately to the Ambassadors at London, but Roosevelt had other contacts not shared by his Secretaries of State. His favorite channel of communication with Britain was Cecil Spring Rice. "Springy" had been Second Secretary at the British Embassy at Washington when Roosevelt served as chairman of the Civil Service

---

[14] Huntington Wilson, *Memoirs of An Ex-Diplomat,* p. 162.
[15] Jessup, *Elihu Root, I,* 457.

Commission, and they had become good friends at that time. Spring Rice was Roosevelt's best man when he was married for the second time, and in the succeeding years the two men corresponded frequently.[16] After Roosevelt entered the White House, Spring Rice usually addressed his letters to "Mrs. Roosevelt," in deference to the sensibilities of his Foreign Office superiors, but the letters were intended for Roosevelt and he answered them. Roosevelt considered Springy a key source of information about world politics as well as an important link with the British government. He told George von Lengerke Meyer: "I have gained the most valuable information from him — better information than I have ever gained from any of our own people abroad, save only Harry White."[17] Liaison through Springy with London was handicapped, however, by the fact that he was seldom at London. He was at the British Embassy at St. Petersburg during the Russo-Japanese War and then went to the isolated post of Minister to Persia. When Roosevelt wished to send an "unofficial" message to the British government he often chose a more direct channel. The one used most often besides Springy was Arthur Lee, a Member of Parliament whom Roosevelt had met in Cuba during the heady days of the Spanish-American War. Lee had been a British military attaché and was an honorary member of the Rough Riders. Roosevelt also corresponded extensively with other men in Britain who were in or near the government, among them George Otto Trevelyan; John St. Loe Strachey, editor of the *Spectator;* Arthur Balfour, who was Prime Minister until the end of 1905; and Sir Edward Grey, who became Foreign Secretary in 1906. He also exchanged letters occasionally with King Edward VII.

Roosevelt's frequent reliance on contacts in London for communication with Britain was partially a result of his inability to deal effectively with Sir Henry Mortimer Durand, who came to Washington as Ambassador in 1903 after the death of Roosevelt's good friend,

---

[16] Roosevelt's friendship with Spring Rice is discussed in Nelson M. Blake, "Ambassadors at the Court of Theodore Roosevelt," *Mississippi Valley Historical Review, XLII* (1955–1956), pp. 179–206.

[17] Roosevelt to Meyer, December 26, 1904, Morison, *Roosevelt Letters, IV,* 1079.

Ambassador Michael Herbert. Durand had little diplomatic experience, having gained fame in the British service in India, and he was a stiff Nineteenth Century Britisher, not at all the type to hit it off with the young President. The incongruity of their relationship is apparent in a letter Durand wrote after an afternoon with Roosevelt in Rock Creek Park:[18]

> Since I wrote I have, to my sorrow, seen something of the President. He invited me to lunch, was very pleasant, and asked me to come back later for a walk. We drove out to the Rock Creek, a wooded valley with a stream running through it, and he then plunged down the *khud,* and made me struggle through bushes and over rocks for two hours and a half, at an impossible speed, till I was so done that I could hardly stand. His great delight is rock climbing, which is my weak point. I disgraced myself completely, and my arms and shoulders are still stiff with dragging myself up by roots and ledges. At one place I fairly stuck, and could not get over the top till he caught me by the collar and hauled at me. He is certainly a "strenuous" man all through. He was dripping with sweat, his clothes frayed by the rocks and bushes and covered with dirt, but he was as happy as a schoolboy. . . . He did almost all the talking, to my great relief, for I had no breath to spare.

Actually Roosevelt's difficulties with Durand did not result primarily from the Ambassador's inability to climb rocks, nor from Roosevelt's desire to have Spring Rice named Ambassador. Durand was ill-suited to the profession of diplomacy and this the Foreign Office itself eventually acknowledged. Roosevelt was of course anxious that Springy be sent when and if he could dislodge Durand. In 1905 he indicated informally to the British government through Ambassador Reid that he would be pleased to have Spring Rice sent as Ambassador;[19] and when Lodge visited London that year Roosevelt told him to "dwell upon the good qualities of Spring Rice" if King Edward or Foreign Secretary Lansdowne opened the subject.[20]

---

[18] Durand to Foreign Secretary Lansdowne, May 17, 1904, Lansdowne Papers, F.O. 800/144, Public Record Office, London, England; Sir Percy M. Sykes, *The Right Honourable Sir Mortimer Durand* (London: Cassell and Co. Ltd., 1926), pp. 275–276.

[19] Roosevelt to Reid, June 5 and 30, 1905, Morison, *Roosevelt Letters, IV,* 1206, 1257–1258.

[20] Roosevelt to Lodge, June 5, 1905, Morison, *Roosevelt Letters, IV,* 1204.

Many months passed before Roosevelt secured Durand's recall. Meanwhile he became increasingly dissatisfied with the Ambassador, and he believed his dissatisfaction was shared by Root, French Ambassador Jusserand, and German Ambassador Speck von Sternburg. During the negotiations over the Moroccan question in 1905 and early 1906 he found Durand "entirely incompetent for any work of delicacy and importance." After the Algeciras conference, he wrote Ambassador Reid:[21]

> It would have been a good thing if I could have kept in touch with England through Durand. But Root and I, and for the matter of that Jusserand and Speck also, have absolutely given up any effort to work with Durand at all. He seems to have a brain of about eight-guinea-pig-power.

In the fall of 1906 Roosevelt renewed the campaign to secure Durand's recall, and the Foreign Office now recognized that Roosevelt was right in thinking Durand unfit for diplomatic work.[22] By this time Roosevelt had all but given up hope that Spring Rice would be appointed, and he mentioned Arthur Lee for the post;[23] but the British government appointed instead James Bryce, a distinguished man of letters who had written a classic work on United States institutions and government entitled *The American Commonwealth*. Bryce was well qualified to fill the post, but there never developed between him and Roosevelt a close relationship like that between the President and the Ambassadors of France and Germany.[24]

Among the foreign diplomats at Washington, French Ambassador

---

[21] Roosevelt to Reid, April 28, 1906, Morison, *Roosevelt Letters, V*, 242, 251.

[22] Sir Edward Grey to Roosevelt, December 4, 1906, Roosevelt Papers. Sir Charles Hardinge, who became Permanent Under Secretary at the Foreign Office in 1906, may have convinced Foreign Secretary Grey that Durand was not suited to the diplomatic service. He had served under Durand in Persia, where Sir Mortimer's unbending manner and laziness had greatly irritated both the Persians and the British Legation staff. Lord Hardinge, *Old Diplomacy: The Reminiscences of Lord Hardinge of Penshurst* (London: J. Murray, 1947), p. 62.

[23] Roosevelt to Reid, November 6, 1906, Morison, *Roosevelt Letters, V*, 488.

[24] Bryce's activities are recounted in H. A. L. Fisher, *James Bryce (Viscount Bryce of Dechmont, O. M.)*, 2 vols. (New York: The Macmillan Co., 1927), *II*, 1–36. It was Hardinge who suggested Bryce for the Washington post. Hardinge, *Old Diplomacy*, pp. 130–132.

Jusserand was the President's most frequent companion. Roosevelt's friendship with German Ambassador Sternburg was more long-standing and perhaps equally strong, but it was Jusserand who graced the tennis cabinet and spent hours at the White House in intellectual discussions with the President. Jusserand was the author of the well-known *English Wayfaring Life in the Middle Ages,* as well as other works of history and literature, and Roosevelt enjoyed his company immensely. In ohe sitting the two could range over such topics as wayfaring life in the Middle Ages, wayfaring life in Colorado, Chaucer, Piers Plowman, Petrarch, Venezuela, and the Hague Tribunal.[25]

Jusserand sent long reports to his government about Roosevelt, explaining that he did so because the influence, the activity, and the power of the President "which drew people to him" were so great that there was nothing insignificant about anything that concerned him. Among other things the Ambassador reported to the Quai d'Orsay his astonishment that Roosevelt did not read the newspapers. "When one knows what one wants," the President had told him, "one must not read the newspapers. It is a useless way of making yourself tired." He was equally amazed that Roosevelt could reserve for himself a large amount of time for all sorts of historical and literary reading, reading not the usual sort for a man with so many responsibilities. Jusserand did his best to place in Roosevelt's hands favorable information to read about France, for he believed that, though the President was not without sincere sympathy for France, he knew it poorly. What reading he had done on France had revealed the skeptical, decadent, quarrelsome sides of French character. Jusserand reported to Paris that it was not difficult, however, to get Roosevelt to see the better side of France, for he was open-minded and of naturally liberal disposition. Jusserand's task was made easy by the fact that Mrs. Roosevelt, who in the eyes of the President was "the model of women and of wives," was of French descent. Madame Jusserand, who was also graced with charming qualities, aided her husband in enlightening the President. Once when Roosevelt ex-

---

[25] Blake, "Ambassadors at the Court of Theodore Roosevelt," *Mississippi Valley Historical Review,* XLII (1955–1956), pp. 192–193.

pounded at length on the German qualities of bravery revealed in the *Nibelungen,* the Ambassadress immediately pointed out that there was nothing in the *Nibelungen* that was particularly German and that the President could find just as much courage and more poetry in the *Song of Roland.* Roosevelt thereupon borrowed a copy from Jusserand, and when next they met, the President was overflowing with enthusiasm for the French epic. Jusserand regretted that he had not reread it before loaning it, for Roosevelt insisted on discussing it with such precision that the Ambassador was at a considerable disadvantage.[26]

In attempting to court the good will of Roosevelt and the American people, Jusserand found himself in constant competition with the Germans. He reported to Paris, with obvious irritation, that German Ambassador Sternburg not only maintained his friendship with Roosevelt but sought to prove the existence of it at every turn. He believed Sternburg was naturally reserved and little used to speech-making, yet he traveled more and gave more speeches than any of his diplomatic colleagues. Added to Sternburg's activities were those of the German Emperor, who multiplied attentions, compliments, praises, and gifts. In 1904 Jusserand reported that William II had sent a statue of Frederick the Great in order to get even with France for sending one of Rochambeau. He also noted that the Germans were attempting to convince the Americans that they had given just as much aid and sympathy as the French during the Revolutionary War and were trying to make Steuben into a second Lafayette. In 1905 Jusserand reported that in one five-week period the Germans had offered the University of St. Louis a bust of William II, offered the University of Chicago a bust of William II and another of Frederick the Great, proposed an exchange of professors between German and American universities, invited American clergymen to the dedication of the Protestant Cathedral in Berlin, offered sociological documents to Harvard University, and purchased land for a new German Embassy. The last item particularly bothered Jusserand, for his quarters were inferior to the existing Ger-

---

[26] Jusserand to Foreign Minister Théophile Delcassé, March 9, 1904, and January 25, 1905, France, Ministère des Affaires Etrangères, *Documents Diplomatique Francais (1871–1914),* 2nd. series (Paris: Imprimerie Nationale, 1930–1955), *IV,* 443–448; *VI,* 61–64.

man Embassy. France had purchased land for a new Embassy, but funds for construction were lacking. Jusserand said that all France had was a vacant lot on which the trees were dying one after the other. Now Germany was preparing to build a new Embassy, and to make matters worse, the new German lot was adjacent to the vacant French plot and was on higher ground.[27]

Neither Jusserand nor his government attempted to compete with the Germans by using the same tactics. Jusserand did some traveling and speech-making, but he thought it appropriate for an Ambassador to maintain some reserve. He therefore declined many invitations to speak and receive honorary degrees. Moreover, he did not think the German activity entirely successful. He conceded that the Americans liked flattery, but he believed the Germans repeated themselves a bit too often. He assured Paris — and his words could not have been more accurate — that in case of serious difficulties it was quite doubtful that the German attentions would change very much the course of events.[28] Jusserand could have added that his own friendship with the President was sufficiently strong that there was little reason for his government to be overly concerned about German activities. However much Roosevelt admired Sternburg, he liked Jusserand just as much and spent far more time with him. While the German Ambassador might be at the University of Pennsylvania delivering a lecture on German colonies, more likely than not Jusserand would be with Roosevelt trekking through Rock Creek Park.

In his memoirs Jusserand affectionately entitled one of his chapters "Walks with Roosevelt" and told of the strenuous hikes with the members of the tennis cabinet. It is a tale of rocks, brambles, thorns, winter snow, and mud holes into which one deliberately stumbled knee-deep. Jusserand quickly learned that one must always go over or through obstacles, never around them. Rock Creek Park and the Potomac were often focal points of the day's adventure, the President usually plunging into the water with clothes on, even when winter ice

---

[27] Jusserand to Delcassé, March 9, 1904, and March 6, 1905, *Documents Diplomatique Francais*, 2nd. series, *IV*, 443–448; *VI*, 172–173.

[28] Jusserand to Delcassé, March 9, 1904, and March 6, 1905, *Documents Diplomatique Francais*, 2nd. series, *IV*, 443–448; *VI*, 172–173.

was floating down the stream. Jusserand recounts how on one rainy day the group rowed across the Potomac in a leaky boat. Midstream Roosevelt struck a dramatic pose, and passing his arm around Jusserand's neck he exclaimed: "Washington and Rochambeau crossing the Delaware!" Summer jaunts were pursued with zest, despite the heat of the capital city. Once in May Roosevelt suggested a swim in the Potomac to cool off, whereupon the troop disrobed completely and dived in. Jusserand, who was wearing kid gloves to protect his hands from the thorns and sharp rocks of the cliffs, forgot to remove them. "Eh, Mr. Ambassador, have you forgotten your gloves?" said Roosevelt. "We might," replied Jusserand, "meet ladies!"[29] Such wit endeared the Ambassador to the President. When Roosevelt left the White House in March 1909, he had a luncheon for the tennis cabinet, and in an impromptu speech on that occasion he declared that there had never been such a relation between an ambassador and a head of government as there had been between Jusserand and himself, that the help and courage which the Ambassador imparted to him at times could not be estimated.[30]

Jusserand was, of course, Roosevelt's most important link with the French government. This was especially true during 1901–1907 when the post of United States Ambassador at Paris was held successively by General Horace Porter and Robert S. McCormick, men who were not among Roosevelt's personal favorites in the diplomatic service. In the fall of 1907, however, Henry White was named Ambassador to France, thus giving Roosevelt another close contact with the French government. "Harry" was regarded by the President as the most useful man in the entire diplomatic service.[31] He had served as Secretary at the Embassy in London when Hay was Ambassador there, and after Hay became Secretary of State, White was his chief source of information in London. A stream of confidential

---

[29] Jusserand, *What Me Befell,* pp. 329–336.

[30] Archie Butt to Mrs. Lewis F. B. Butt, March 1, 1909, Lawrence F. Abbott (ed.), *The Letters of Archie Butt, Personal Aide to President Roosevelt* (New York: Doubleday, Page, and Co., 1924), pp. 368–369.

[31] Allan Nevins, *Henry White: Thirty Years of American Diplomacy* (New York: Harper & Bros., 1930), pp. 305–306.

letters flowed between the two men until Hay's death in 1905. In that year White was named Ambassador to Italy, a post from which he sent long informative letters to both Roosevelt and Root. In the following year he served as chief United States delegate to the Algeciras conference, and then in 1907 was appointed to the Paris post. While in France White exchanged long letters with Roosevelt, though happily there were no important disputes in Franco-American relations which required their attention. Much of the correspondence soon centered upon Roosevelt's trip to Africa and Europe, which he planned to take when he left the White House. White shared Roosevelt's enthusiasm for the trip, but by the time it occurred White was no longer Ambassador at Paris. He had been unceremoniously ousted from the diplomatic service by Taft, the new President, an act which Roosevelt bitterly resented.[32]

Roosevelt's chief diplomatic channel to Berlin during almost his entire time in the White House was his old friend Speck von Sternburg. Roosevelt was hardly in the White House before he was telling the German Kaiser, William II, that "it would be very agreeable to me to have Speck sent back to Washington." [33] Sternburg had been a Secretary at the German Embassy in Washington when Roosevelt was chairman of the Civil Service Commission and Spring Rice was at the British Embassy, and the three men developed a lasting friendship. The Kaiser was quite willing to take advantage of this personal connection, and he soon sent Sternburg to Washington as Ambassador. Meanwhile Charlemagne Tower was sent as United States Ambassador to Berlin. This latter appointment proved very agreeable to William II but of little use to Roosevelt. Tower fell so completely under the sway of the Kaiser's charms that Roosevelt regarded him as unreliable. The President therefore relied almost completely upon Sternburg in his dealings with Germany. Specky did not become a member of the tennis cabinet, but he occasionally went horseback riding with the President and frequently visited the White House. Roosevelt's esteem for him was so great that when

---

[32] Nevins, *Henry White,* pp. 298–299, 305–306.

[33] Roosevelt to Andrew D. White, December 17, 1901, Morison, *Roosevelt Letters, III,* 208.

Sternburg died in 1908 he told Henry White that he had never met a man for whom he had a higher respect or regard.[34]

As friend and confidant, Roosevelt's assessment of Speck was well deserved, but unfortunately in terms of being a capable and effective diplomat the German Ambassador did not merit high marks. Sternburg, for all his sincerity and good intentions, was constantly misinforming his government about Roosevelt's attitudes and policies; and concurrently he was unwittingly misleading Roosevelt about his own government's position. His misinterpretation of his instructions during the Moroccan crisis — pledging the Kaiser to let Roosevelt determine German policy — was the worst case of his diplomatic ineptitude, but it was only one instance of a condition that was chronic. Sir Eyre Crowe was, if anything, understating the case when he said that Sternburg was "not a man of any real ability." [35]

Some of the blame for Sternburg's inaccurate reports from Washington to Berlin — which have misled historians almost as much as they misled the Kaiser — must be laid at the feet of Roosevelt. The President knew the Kaiser's susceptibility to flattery, and he used it lavishly in order to influence the gullible German. Also, because of his friendship with Specky, Roosevelt always spoke in polite and friendly language even when expounding policy that ran counter to Germany's interest. If Roosevelt had realized the extent of the Ambassador's misrepresentation of his views, he doubtless would have spoken with more clarity and frankness, and he should have done so in any case. Sternburg nevertheless should have evaluated with more discernment the attitudes and policies of the government to which he was accredited. In the Roosevelt-Sternburg relationship friendship proved to be a greater hindrance than an aid to effective diplomatic exchange.

Roosevelt found communicating effectively with Berlin difficult; with St. Petersburg he found it almost impossible. Count Arturo Cassini, who was Ambassador at Washington until the end of the

[34] Roosevelt to White, September 10, 1908, Morison, *Roosevelt Letters, VI*, 1230.

[35] Note by Crowe attached to Sir Frank Lascelles to Sir Edward Grey, telegram, August 24, 1908, F.O. 371/461, Public Record Office.

Russo-Japanese War, lied so consistently to Hay and Roosevelt that they learned to put no credence whatever in anything he said. "What I cannot understand about the Russian," Roosevelt exclaimed to Senator Lodge with a feeling of bewilderment, "is the way he will lie when he knows perfectly well that you know he is lying." [36] By the time Roosevelt undertook to arrange the peace conference between Russia and Japan, he had just about given up having any dealings with the Russian Ambassador. Roosevelt was further handicapped by having an Ambassador at St. Petersburg that he considered unreliable. Robert S. McCormick, who filled that post until the spring of 1905, was so pro-Russian that it caused comment among the diplomats in the Russian capital,[37] this at a time when Russia was doing nothing to deserve American good will. Roosevelt obtained much good information from Spencer Eddy, the First Secretary of the Embassy, but he needed someone at the head of the mission who could deal effectively with Russian leaders. In March 1905 he found the right man for the post. He transferred McCormick to Paris and sent George von Lengerke Meyer to St. Petersburg. The appointment came at the moment that Roosevelt was preparing to play a key role in peacemaking between Russia and Japan, and he expected Meyer to participate in that endeavor. When Roosevelt informed Meyer of his appointment, he told him he wanted some work done:[38]

> The trouble with our Ambassadors in stations of real importance is that they totally fail to give us real help and real information, and seem to think that the life work of an Ambassador is a kind of glorified pink tea party. Now, at St. Petersburg I want some work done, and you are the man to do it.

Happily Meyer fulfilled all Roosevelt's expectations. After Meyer had been at the post for a few months, Roosevelt told him that Hay had received from Spencer Eddy, "a letter of wild enthusiasm contrasting

---

[36] Roosevelt to Lodge, June 16, 1905, Morison, *Roosevelt Letters, IV,* 1232.

[37] Spring Rice to Mrs. Roosevelt, May 25, 1904, Stephen Gwynn, *The Letters and Friendships of Sir Cecil Spring Rice: A Record,* 2 vols. (Boston and New York: Houghton Mifflin Co., 1929), *I,* 410.

[38] Roosevelt to Meyer, December 26, 1904, Morison, *Roosevelt Letters, IV,* 1078–1080.

you with McCormick." [39] Even with a capable Ambassador at St. Petersburg, however, it was difficult to communicate with the amorphous Russian government. During the negotiations ending the Russo-Japanese War, therefore, Roosevelt had Meyer deliver messages not to the Foreign Ministry but directly to the Tsar, a task Meyer handled with consummate skill.

Roosevelt's personal contacts with diplomats dealing with Far Eastern affairs were limited and not as intimate as with those handling European matters. He had talks with Kogoro Takahira, who served at Washington as Minister during 1900–1906 and returned as Ambassador in 1908. The only period when Roosevelt saw Takahira frequently, however, was during the Russo-Japanese War. Hay, Roosevelt, and Root liked Takahira and marveled at his command of English. Hay wrote to Roosevelt in 1903:[40]

> See what a remarkable letter this is from Takahira. Even when he misspelled a word — 'indefateguable' he has an etymological reason for it. Yet Jusserand says that Takahira cannot write English. I wish I could write any foreign language as well.

After the conclusion of the Portsmouth Peace Conference, Roosevelt told Takahira that he considered him a man with so high a standard of honor and integrity that he could put absolute trust in him and that consequently he had been able to deal with him with a freedom and frankness "rare as between two representatives of even the most friendly nations." [41]

Roosevelt also had talks with Baron Kentaro Kaneko, Japan's special envoy in the United States during the Russo-Japanese War. The importance of Kaneko's part in the diplomacy of the war and the peace conference, however, has been generally overrated. Roosevelt mistakenly treated him as having full authority to serve as liaison between himself and the Japanese government, but neither Takahira nor Foreign Minister Jutaro Komura considered his activities impor-

---

[39] Roosevelt to Meyer, July 7, 1905, Morison, *Roosevelt Letters, IV*, 1262–1263.

[40] Hay to Roosevelt, August 19, 1903, John Hay Papers, Library of Congress, Washington, D. C.

[41] Roosevelt to Takahira, September 8, 1905, Roosevelt Papers.

tant and they placed little confidence in him. Kaneko probably confused more than he aided communication between Roosevelt and the Japanese government.[42]

Roosevelt's relations with Siuzo Aoki, who was Ambassador at Washington during 1906–1907, were unusually cordial, though the two men conferred infrequently. Roosevelt and Root liked Aoki so much that when he got into a quarrel with Foreign Minister Tadasu Hayashi, they endeavored — though unsuccessfully — to prevent his recall.[43]

At the Tokyo post Roosevelt had able men, but he did not often deal with them directly. Lloyd Griscom, who served as Minister to Japan before and during the Russo-Japanese War, was considered by Roosevelt to be one of the few able diplomats to come up through the ranks of the career service.[44] When the post at Tokyo was raised to ambassadorial level in 1908, Roosevelt named Luke E. Wright of Tennessee as Ambassador, an appointment made largely to groom Wright for a cabinet position. When Wright resigned in 1907, Thomas James O'Brien was sent to the Tokyo post. O'Brien was probably the ablest of the three men who served at Tokyo during the Roosevelt administration. He, like his predecessors Griscom and Wright, however, seldom received letters from the President. Roosevelt gained some information from the official dispatches from Tokyo, but except for the period of the Russo-Japanese War, he did not closely follow the official correspondence other than that relating to the Japanese immigration problem.

William W. Rockhill, whom Roosevelt named Minister to Peking in 1905, likewise received letters only infrequently from the President. Rockhill had been Hay's chief adviser on Far Eastern affairs. He was a renowned scholar on Mongolia and Tibet and had, along with A. E. Hippisley, drafted the famous open door notes of 1899. Yet, once Rockhill was sent to China as Minister, Roosevelt treated him more like a distinguished scholarly ornament than a diplomat who might

---

[42] Esthus, *Theodore Roosevelt and Japan,* pp. 90–91.

[43] Esthus, *Theodore Roosevelt and Japan,* pp. 208–209.

[44] Roosevelt to Francis Cabot Lowell, January 8, 1906, Morison, *Roosevelt Letters,* V, 129–130.

keep him posted on Far Eastern matters. Root kept in close touch with Rockhill through the official correspondence, but there is no evidence that much of the information in Rockhill's dispatches reached Roosevelt. As a result, except for the nineteen-month period of the Russo-Japanese War, Roosevelt was poorly informed about the Far East. He kept a keen eye on the Japanese problems at home — the Japanese immigration question and the mistreatment of Japanese aliens in California — but he did not follow closely developments west of Hawaii. Hay, before the Russo-Japanese War, and Root, after the Russo-Japanese War, were far better informed than Roosevelt concerning the problems of East Asia. The President's personal diplomatic contacts remained almost completely Europe-oriented.

Such contacts as Roosevelt had with the diplomats gave to his diplomacy, at least on the surface, a strong personal character. Personal diplomacy by Presidents has not always resulted in efficient handling of foreign affairs, but in Roosevelt's case there seems to have been more advantage than disadvantage. Unlike Woodrow Wilson and Franklin Roosevelt, whose personal diplomacy involved the vital interests of the United States, Theodore Roosevelt's personal diplomacy related almost exclusively to the vital interests of other nations. But whether his personal diplomacy was gain or loss, it could not have been impersonal. It was a reflection of his own exuberant personality, ecumenical interests, and boyish enthusiasm to be at the center of things. He enjoyed immensely the personal contacts with the diplomats, both in the serious business of diplomacy and in hiking with Jusserand or riding with Sternburg. Moreover, his friendships provided him with informal channels with which to play the part of world leader.

Personal diplomacy was to some extent, of course, a two-way street. If it provided Roosevelt convenient instruments with which to engage in the game of international politics, it also gave other governments opportunities to influence the American President. It would be easy, however, to overestimate the influence of the diplomats upon Roosevelt. Had it not been for his friendship with Sternburg he doubtless would have been more anti-German than he was, but even with Specky's friendly influence Roosevelt's policy was consistently anti-German. Conversely, when Roosevelt was irritated at the British for not sending Spring Rice as Ambassador, his policy was nevertheless strongly pro-British. At that time Secretary of War Taft assured the Japanese Prime Minister that the United States was so fully in accord with the policy of the Anglo-Japanese Alliance that cooperation could be counted on as if the United States were under treaty obligations, a view in which Roosevelt enthusiastically concurred.[45] Jusserand inclined the President to be more friendly to France than he otherwise would have been, but this was probably of little significance. In the Moroccan crisis of 1905–1906 Roosevelt sided with France completely, but it would be impossible to substantiate the theory that Jusserand was responsible for this. Roosevelt was so firmly convinced that a civilized nation should take over the wretched country of Morocco that his policy probably would have been strongly pro-French without Jusserand's influence. Despite all of Roosevelt's sincere attachments to the diplomats, it is very doubtful that any of them ever exercised a decisive influence upon him.

---

[45] Esthus, *Theodore Roosevelt and Japan,* pp. 102–104.

The Balance of Power in East Asia

2

The mainspring of Theodore Roosevelt's Far Eastern policy in the years from 1901 to 1905 was the desire to establish a balance of power in East Asia. He believed that it was to the interest of all nations, Eastern and Western, that a balance of power exist in that troubled area of the world. This balance he envisaged principally in terms of Russia and Japan, for China was contemptibly weak and the Western powers, with their principal strategic interests elsewhere on the globe, could have only limited interests in East Asia.

When Roosevelt entered the White House in 1901, conditions in East Asia were badly out of joint. During 1896–1899 Germany, Russia, France, and Britain had carved out spheres of influence in China, and the Boxer Rebellion of 1900 brought such chaos that the complete partitionment of China appeared imminent. As it turned out, however, only Russia in 1900 represented a serious threat to China's integrity. During the rebellion fifty thousand Russian troops had poured into Manchuria, and in the subsequent years St. Petersburg attempted to make the grip on the Three Eastern Provinces permanent. The need for a balance of power in East Asia became painfully manifest to Roosevelt in 1902–1903 as Russian influence not only pervaded Manchuria but threatened to spread south beyond the Great Wall to Peking, the capital of the Celestial Empire.

As early as 1900 Roosevelt envisaged Japan as the logical counterpoise to Russian power in East Asia. In that year he confided to Speck von Sternburg that it would be best if Japan held Korea so that it might be a check upon Russia.[1] This was a role the Tokyo government was not averse to filling, but for three years it attempted to roll back the Russians peacefully. In 1902 Japan concluded an alliance with Britain which would guarantee it against the intervention of a third power in a Russo-Japanese War (Britain pledging military assistance if Japan became involved in war with more than one enemy while defending Japanese interests in Korea and China). Then in the summer of 1903 Japan opened comprehensive negotiations with Russia. As those negotiations progressed, however, it became increasingly apparent that the diplomatic leverage provided by the Anglo-Japanese Alliance and by Japan's own war preparations would be insufficient to dislodge the Russians.

While Japan prepared to take up the Russian challenge by force of arms if necessary, the United States pursued a cautious policy. The American public simply would not support a policy which envisaged American power as a counterbalance to Russia in East Asia. As Secretary of State John Hay reminded Roosevelt in April 1903:[2]

> I take it for granted that Russia knows as well as we do that we will not fight over Manchuria, for the simple reason that we cannot. . . . If our rights and our interests in opposition to Russia in the Far East were as clear as noonday, we could never get a treaty through the Senate the object of which was to check Russian aggression.

With no strong cards to play in the Far East, Roosevelt turned his attention largely to the Caribbean. Hay was thus left to salvage what he could from the China mess. While Secretary of State under President McKinley, he had enunciated the twin principles of America's Far Eastern policy, the open door for commerce and the integrity of China. Now under Roosevelt he sought to preserve the open door

---

[1] Roosevelt to Sternburg, August 28, 1900, Elting E. Morison (ed.), *The Letters of Theodore Roosevelt*, 8 vols. (Cambridge, Mass.: Harvard University Press, 1951–1954), *II*, 1394.

[2] Hay to Roosevelt, April 28, 1903, John Hay Papers, Library of Congress, Washington, D. C.

even if it meant forsaking the concept of China's integrity. In negotiating with Russia he showed a willingness to recognize Russia's "exceptional position" in Manchuria if he could obtain assurances in return that "no matter what happens eventually in northern China and Manchuria, the United States shall not be placed in any worse position than while the country was under the unquestioned domination of China." [3]

Roosevelt gave only fitful attention to the Far East before the outbreak of the Russo-Japanese War, but when he did turn his thoughts eastward, he voiced great irritation at Russian behavior. In the summer of 1903 he told Hay that he was thoroughly aroused at Russia's conduct in Manchuria, that he did not intend to give way, and that he was growing more confident that the American public would back him in "going to an extreme in the matter." [4] In his calmer moments, though, he must have known that Hay's assessment of the American public was correct, for his strong words were not matched by deeds. Actually, the decisive rivalry that was shaping up in East Asia in 1903 was not the Russian-American rivalry but the Russo-Japanese rivalry, for the Russian descent upon China threatened Japan's interests far more than it threatened American interests.

Japanese leaders were convinced by the fall of 1903 that Russian troops must be removed from Manchuria, even if it meant throwing them out by force of arms. Otherwise Russian power would spread over Korea and constitute an intolerable menace to Japan's security. In the negotiations with Russia in 1903 Japan found that the St. Petersburg government would agree to nothing that would recognize Chinese territorial integrity in regard to Manchuria. Furthermore, the Japanese were led to believe that Russia would also insist upon a "neutral zone" in North Korea, an area in which Russian influence would probably prevail.[5] In February 1904, after six months of fruitless negotiations, Japan severed relations and launched a surprise

---

[3] Hay to Roosevelt, May 1, 1902, Theodore Roosevelt Papers, Library of Congress, Washington, D. C.

[4] Roosevelt to Hay, July 18, 1903, Morison, *Roosevelt Letters, III,* 520.

[5] Raymond A. Esthus, *Theodore Roosevelt and Japan* (Seattle, Wash.: University of Washington Press, 1966), pp. 13–22.

attack on Russian naval forces at Port Arthur, the port in South Manchuria which Russia had leased from China in 1898.

At the outbreak of the war Roosevelt was strongly pro-Japanese. When news came of the Japanese naval victory at Port Arthur, he wrote to his son, Theodore Roosevelt, Jr., "I was thoroughly well pleased with the Japanese victory, for Japan is playing our game." [6] What pleased Roosevelt most was that Japan's victory indicated that Japan would likely establish itself as an effective counterbalance to Russian power in East Asia. News of further Japanese victories in the succeeding weeks appeared to confirm this. In fact, Japanese arms were so successful that Roosevelt's elation was soon mixed with apprehension. If Russian power were thoroughly shattered, then there would be no force to counterbalance Japan.

Roosevelt did not wish to see Japan defeated — he even intended to help it retain the fruits of victory if the powers intervened to oppose reasonable Japanese gains — but he certainly did not wish the Japanese to win too overwhelmingly. In the second month of the war he wrote to Spring Rice that if the Japanese won, not only Russia but all the powers would have to reckon with a "great new force in eastern Asia." He went on to express the thought that the two powers might fight until both were fairly well exhausted and that peace would come on terms which would not mean the creation of "either a yellow peril, or a Slav peril." [7] In the same month he told German Ambassador Sternburg that it was to the interest of the powers that the war between Russia and Japan should drag on, "so that both powers may exhaust themselves as much as possible and that their geographical area of friction should not be eliminated after the conclusion of peace." [8] Where Roosevelt wanted the geographical line between Russian and Japanese power was apparent three months

---

[6] Roosevelt to Theodore Roosevelt, Jr., February 10, 1904, Morison, *Roosevelt Letters, IV,* 724.

[7] Roosevelt to Spring Rice, March 19, 1904, Morison, *Roosevelt Letters, IV,* 759–761.

[8] Sternburg to the Foreign Office, telegram, March 21, 1904, Germany, Auswärtiges Amt, *Die Grosse Politik der Europäischen Kabinette, 1871–1914,* 40 vols. (Berlin: Deutsche verlagagesellschaft für politik und geschichte, 1922–1927), *XIX,* 112–113.

later when he told Japanese leaders quite frankly that he hoped their armies would not go north of Mukden in South Manchuria.[9]

As the Japanese won further victories Roosevelt continued to worry that Russian power would be completely destroyed in Eastern Asia. In a talk with Sternburg in December 1904, he observed that it was to the advantage of Germany and the United States that Japan should succeed "but not too overwhelmingly."[10] More Japanese victories in 1905 led Roosevelt to believe that the armies of the Mikado were well-nigh invincible. Port Arthur fell in January. Two months later came the gigantic Battle of Mukden in which Russian forces were routed with a loss of 97,000 men.

Though Roosevelt did not realize it, the Battle of Mukden established the balance of power which he so fervently desired. Japan had reached the limit of its military and financial capacity. In the wake of that battle, Japanese forces would penetrate slightly north of Mukden, and later Japanese naval supremacy would permit the capture of the island of Sakhalin, but the Japanese armies could not annihilate the Russian forces in Manchuria. Japanese military leaders were even doubtful that they could win another great battle. Indeed, the Battle of Mukden was hardly over before Japan's highest military leaders were insisting to the civilian leaders in Tokyo that peace must be made.[11]

While Japanese military leaders demanded peace, the Japanese government unwisely took a step that went directly counter to that objective. It expanded its war aims to include an indemnity and cession of the island of Sakhalin. For these new terms Roosevelt betrayed no enthusiasm. What worried him most was that they would make Russia more reluctant to make peace and thus prolong the war. He feared that if the war continued disaster might overtake either side and the possibility of a balance of power would be totally de-

---

[9] Takahira to Komura, June 9, 1904, Telegram Series, *XLI*, 1959–1962, Japanese Ministry of Foreign Affairs Archives, microfilm collection, Library of Congress, Washington, D. C.

[10] Hay diary, December 6, 1904, Hay Papers.

[11] Tatsuji Takeuchi, *War and Diplomacy in the Japanese Empire* (New York: Doubleday, Doran & Co., 1935), p. 149.

stroyed. The Russian Baltic fleet was approaching the theater of war and there was at least a chance that it might smash the Japanese fleet and thus cut the supply line to the Japanese armies in Manchuria. More likely, Japan would win a spectacular victory at sea and go on to wipe out Russian forces in all Eastern Asia. "Personally I wish that Japan had made peace on the conditions she originally thought of after Mukden was fought," Roosevelt wrote anxiously to Spring Rice on May 13, 1905.[12]

The naval encounter came on May 28, 1905, near the island of Tsushima in the Korean Strait. It was a decisive Japanese victory, all eight Russian battleships being sunk or captured while Japan lost not a single ship. Yet it opened the way not to the Japanese conquest of eastern Siberia but to peace negotiations. At the moment of victory Japan requested Roosevelt "directly and entirely on his own motion and initiative" to invite Russia and Japan to undertake direct negotiations. In the subsequent days Roosevelt wrung from Tsar Nicholas reluctant assent to open peace negotiations. Several weeks were consumed in arranging the details of the conference, but Roosevelt was finally able to announce that Japan would send Foreign Minister Jutaro Komura and Takahira to the negotiations, that Russia would send Serge Witte and Baron Rosen, and that the conference would open in Washington, D. C., in the first ten days of August. Before that date the site was shifted to a cooler location, the United States naval base at Kittery, Maine, adjacent to Portsmouth, New Hampshire.

Japan's initiative to bring about a peace conference should have given Roosevelt a clue that Japan's capacity to win further major victories was probably not as great as he had thought and that the balance of power already existed, but he did not perceive this. He was convinced that if the war continued, Japan could drive Russia completely out of East Asia. If the Japanese maintained the struggle, he wrote to Andrew D. White on June 1, Russia was "certain to go on from disaster to disaster."[13] To Ambassador Whitelaw Reid at Lon-

---

[12] Roosevelt to Spring Rice, May 13, 1905, Morison, *Roosevelt Letters, IV,* 1178–1179.

[13] Roosevelt to White, June 1, 1905, Morison, *Roosevelt Letters, IV,* 1200.

don he wrote: "I should be sorry to see Russia driven out of East Asia, and driven out she surely will be if the war goes on."[14] Later in the same month he wrote to Spring Rice that if the war lasted a year, Japan would drive Russia out of East Asia.[15] To Senator Lodge he observed:[16]

> While Russia's triumph would have been a blow to civilization, her destruction as an eastern Asiatic power would also in my opinion be unfortunate. It is best that she should be left face to face with Japan so that each may have a moderative action on the other.

These views Roosevelt conveyed frankly to the Russian government through Ambassador George von Lengerke Meyer, who had been appointed to the St. Petersburg post the previous March. In a message to Russian leaders, dispatched on June 19, he asserted that Japan had won an overwhelming triumph and that from the Russian standpoint the war was hopeless. If Russia continued to fight in hope of escaping payment of an indemnity, all Eastern Siberia would be lost and Russia would never recover it. It would be far better, he counselled, to make peace by paying a reasonable indemnity and surrendering Sakhalin, for Russia could never redeem itself in the war. "In advising this," said Roosevelt, "I speak for Russia's interest, because on this point Russia's interests are the interests of the world. I do not want to see her driven off the Pacific Slope. . . ."[17]

Although Roosevelt urged Russia to pay an indemnity, he simultaneously warned the Japanese that they should either not press the indemnity claim or seek only a very modest sum. He reminded Takahira that Japan already had Port Arthur and Korea and dominance in Manchuria, and the less it asked in addition the better it would be.[18] His efforts to get Japan to moderate the money demand were moti-

---

[14] Roosevelt to Reid, June 5, 1905, Roosevelt Papers.

[15] Roosevelt to Spring Rice, June 16, 1905, Morison, *Roosevelt Letters, IV,* 1233–1234.

[16] Roosevelt to Lodge, June 16, 1905, Morison, *Roosevelt Letters, IV,* 1230.

[17] Roosevelt to Meyer, June 19, 1905, Morison, *Roosevelt Letters, IV,* 1241–1242.

[18] Roosevelt to Lodge, June 16, 1905, Morison, *Roosevelt Letters, IV,* 1230.

vated primarily by his desire to see the Peace conference succeed. Success was imperative, he believed, if a balance of power was to be achieved. He obviously wished the negotiations to succeed also because the peace conference was his project, but if his private correspondence gives an accurate indication, he was far more concerned about attaining a balance of power than gaining personal fame. Throughout the period immediately preceding the conference and during the conference itself, his principal worry continued to be that the peace effort would fail, the war would continue, and Russian power in East Asia would be thoroughly shattered.

Roosevelt hammered away at the indemnity issue incessantly, but he did not urge upon Japan similar moderation regarding the demand for Sakhalin, the large island north of Japan. This demand he felt was justified.[19] Lodge gave full endorsement to Roosevelt's views in this regard, and the Senator was even more categorical than the President in opposing the indemnity demand. He told Roosevelt that he believed Japan was entitled to Sakhalin and would be justified in refusing to make peace without its cession, but it should not continue the war for an indemnity. "I am bound to say," he commented, "I do not think her case for an indemnity a good one. She holds no Russian territory except Sakhalin, and that she wants to keep." [20] Both Roosevelt and Lodge believed apparently that the demand for Sakhalin would be no insurmountable obstacle to successful peace negotiations. They probably calculated that the cession of a largely uninhabited island which both Russia and Japan had claimed until 1875 would be much less humiliating to the Tsar than the payment of an indemnity. In view of all Japan's victories, it seemed only just to them that while Japan was pressed to forego or greatly moderate the money demand, it not be urged to give up the island claim also.

When the peace conference convened on August 9 Witte and Komura had little difficulty in reaching fundamental agreements

---

[19] Roosevelt to Spring Rice, July 24, 1905, Morison, *Roosevelt Letters, IV,* 1238–1287.

[20] Lodge to Roosevelt, August 21, 1905, *Selections from the Correspondence of Theodore Roosevelt and Henry Cabot Lodge, 1884–1918,* 2 vols. (New York: Charles Scribner's Sons, 1925), *II,* 176–177.

which, in effect, confirmed the balance of power then existing between the opposing armies in Manchuria. During the first nine days of negotiations Russia agreed to recognize Japan's paramount political, military, and economic interests in Korea and to transfer to Japan the Port Arthur leasehold in South Manchuria and the railway stretching from Changchun in central Manchuria to Port Arthur. Both powers agreed to evacuate their armies from Manchuria within eighteen months and restore that area to Chinese administration. Thus by August 18 a peace settlement was emerging which followed almost precisely what Roosevelt envisioned as a suitable postwar balance of power. By that date, however, it had become apparent that these basic agreements might be lost because of a hardening deadlock on the peripheral questions of an indemnity and cession of territory. Tokyo had not instructed Komura to make these latter items "imperative demands," [21] but he was nevertheless intent upon attaining them.

Roosevelt decided to intervene in the negotiations to save them from collapse. From Oyster Bay, where he was spending the summer, he sent a personal appeal to Tsar Nicholas on August 21, urging the acceptance of a compromise plan which Witte and Komura had drafted. Russia would cede the southern half of Sakhalin to Japan and would make a money payment for the return of the northern half. His appeal revealed his continuing anxiety that a balance of power would not be attained. He warned the Tsar bluntly that if Russia did not make peace the east Siberian provinces which Russia had held for centuries would be lost.[22] While appealing to Russia he also sent pleas to Japan urging that only a small sum be asked for the return of northern Sakhalin to Russia.[23]

Roosevelt's appeal to the Tsar kept the conference going and also brought a concession. When the message went to St. Petersburg, it

---

[21] Collection of Cabinet Decisions, PVM 9–55, pp. 1029–1033, Japanese Ministry of Foreign Affairs Archives, microfilm collection, Library of Congress, Washington, D. C.

[22] Roosevelt to Meyer, telegram, August 21, 1905, Morison, *Roosevelt Letters,* V, 4–5.

[23] Roosevelt to Kaneko, August 22 and 23, 1905, Morison, *Roosevelt Letters,* IV, 1308–1310, 1312–1313.

crossed telegrams from the Russian capital instructing Witte to break up the conference, instructions Witte now ignored since Roosevelt's message required a response from the Tsar.[24] In his reply the Tsar agreed to the cession of the southern half of Sakhalin.[25] This was not sufficient, however, to break the deadlock. The Tsar refused to pay any money for the return of northern Sakhalin, and Komura was insistent that Japan secure some kind of monetary payment.

Roosevelt realized that the peace conference was on the verge of collapse; his fears for the balance of power increased. A letter from Senator Lodge underscored his anxieties. It was desirable to secure peace now, said Lodge, for it was not in the interest of the United States or of the world generally that Russia be too completely crippled. "It is better that in the future they [Japan and Russia] should both be strong enough to hold each other in check and keep the peace in the Orient."[26] A few days after receiving this letter, Roosevelt sent a second appeal to the Tsar, this one revealing even more bluntly his fears of future military reverses for Russia. He asserted that in the estimate of most outside observers there was a strong possibility that although Japan would be required to make heavy sacrifices, it could take Harbin, Vladivostok, and East Siberia, and if this were once done the probabilities were overwhelming that it could never be dislodged.[27] The Tsar, however, remained unconvinced. On August 28 he instructed Witte to break up the conference "in any case."[28]

---

[24] Foreign Minister Vladimir Lamsdorff to Witte, telegrams nos. 147, 148, 150, August 9/22, 1905, Witte to Lamsdorff, telegram no. 152, August 9/22, 1905, Ministerstvo inostrannykh del, *Sbornik diplomaticheskikh dokumentov, Kasaiushchikhsia peregovorov mezhdu Rossiei i Iaponiei o zakliuchenii mirnogo dogovora, 24 maia-3 oktiabria, 1905*, St. Petersburg, 1906, pp. 167–170, 170–171.

[25] Meyer to Roosevelt, telegrams, August 23 and 24, 1905, Morison, *Roosevelt Letters, V*, 5–6; M. A. De Wolfe Howe, *George von Lengerke Meyer, His Life and Public Services* (New York: Dodd, Mead & Co.), pp. 197–202.

[26] Lodge to Roosevelt, August 21, 1905, *Selections from the Correspondence of Theodore Roosevelt and Henry Cabot Lodge, II*, 176–177.

[27] Roosevelt to Meyer, telegram, August 25, 1905, Morison, *Roosevelt Letters, IV*, 1314–1315.

[28] Lamsdorff to Witte, telegram no. 180, August 15/28, 1905, *Sbornik diplomatischeskikh dokumentov*, p. 193; Serge Witte, *The Memoirs of Count*

At the eleventh hour Witte saved the peace negotiations despite the order of the Tsar. The Russian negotiator determined to violate his instructions and make peace if Japan would settle for the southern half of Sakhalin with no money payment.[29] Concurrently Tokyo became convinced that Russia intended to break off negotiations and decided to back down. Japan was so desperate for peace that on August 28 the Japanese government instructed Komura to give up both the money claim and the demand for Sakhalin.[30] The retreat on the island issue was most surprising of all, for the Tsar had agreed to cede the southern half of Sakhalin, an offer Witte had repeated formally at Portsmouth. Roosevelt, however, had not informed the Tokyo government of the Tsar's concession, and Komura's messages to Tokyo had not made clear that Witte was offering such a concession at the conference.

As it turned out, Japan achieved peace and secured the southern half of Sakhalin also. At the last minute the Japanese government learned through the British Ambassador at Tokyo that the Tsar had agreed to cede southern Sakhalin in response to Roosevelt's appeal — this news coming from the British Ambassador at St. Petersburg via London. A telegram was hurriedly sent to Komura early on August 29 instructing him to hold out for southern Sakhalin.[31] When the delegates met on that day, Witte and Komura quickly agreed to the compromise in which Japan relinquished the money claim, returned northern Sakhalin to Russia, and received title to southern Sakhalin.[32] Within a few days the diplomats put the finishing touches on the text of their agreement and on September 5 staged the formal signing of the Treaty of Portsmouth.

Witte, translated and edited by Abraham Yarmolinsky (New York: Doubleday Page & Co., 1921), p. 178.

[29] Witte to Lamsdorff, telegram no. 182, August 16/29, 1905, *Sbornik diplomaticheskikh dokumentov,* pp. 193–194.

[30] Prime Minister Taro Katsura to Komura, telegram, August 28, 1905, Japan, Gaimusho, *Komura Gaikoshi,* 2 vols. (Tokyo: Gaimusho, 1953), *II,* 125–126.

[31] Katsura to Komura, telegram, August 29, 1905, *Komura Gaikoshi, II,* 126–127; John A. White, *The Diplomacy of the Russo-Japanese War* (Princeton: Princeton University Press, 1964), pp. 307–308.

[32] J. J. Korostovetz, *Pre-War Diplomacy: The Russo-Japanese Problem, Treaty Signed at Portsmouth, U. S. A., 1905, Diary of J. J. Korostovetz* (London: British Periodicals Ltd., 1920), pp. 106–108.

Roosevelt was surprised at Japan's decision to relinquish both the money claim and northern Sakhalin. He confided to Spring Rice:[33]

> I think the Japanese gave up more than they need to have given up when they returned the northern half of Sakhalin, which I am confident I could have obtained for them — or at least which I think I could have made Russia redeem for a small sum of money.

From what is now known from the Russian records, it is obvious that Roosevelt was mistaken in thinking Japan could have gotten more. The Tsar would not have made any concession, and by August 28 he did not even want peace on the terms he himself had previously approved. There were few times when Nicholas II exhibited good judgment, but he was more perceptive than Roosevelt in sensing the weakness of the Japanese. It is likely that the Tsar's plans for great military victories were on the optimistic side, and there was certainly enough uncertainty over Russia's domestic political conditions to make continuance of the war risky. However, unless all the estimates of the Japanese military leaders were wrong, Roosevelt's belief that Japan could have taken Eastern Siberia was not justified. If the war had continued, it is likely that the military stalemate which had characterized the situation in Manchuria for almost six months would have continued with both sides feeling enormous strains and shouldering great risks. That is to say, the balance of power which came into being with the Battle of Mukden probably would have endured.

Within a few weeks of the signing of the Treaty of Portsmouth, Roosevelt realized that the balance of power had actually been achieved before the peace conference. He wrote to Sturgis Bigelow on September 23 that it was a mistake to think Japan could have easily taken Eastern Siberia. He pointed out that months went by after the Battle of Mukden without the Japanese Army undertaking a major offensive in Manchuria and that the Russian Army had grown stronger during that time.[34] Three weeks later in a letter drafted to

---

[33] Roosevelt to Spring Rice, September 1, 1905, Stephen Gwynn, *The Letters and Friendships of Sir Cecil Spring Rice: A Record*, 2 vols. (Boston and New York: Houghton Mifflin Co., 1929), *I*, 489.

[34] Roosevelt to Bigelow, September 23, 1905, Roosevelt Papers.

George Kennan (but not sent), Roosevelt confessed that he had not appreciated quite how urgently Japan needed peace. He now understood, however, that Japan had reached a point where it lacked both recruits and money.[35]

Meanwhile the riots that broke out in Tokyo in opposition to the treaty reinforced Roosevelt's belief that the Portsmouth Treaty served the interests of the United States. He wrote to Lodge on September 6: "The outbreak in Tokyo is unpleasant evidence that the Japanese mob — I hope not the Japanese people — had its head completely turned; the peace is evidently a wise one from our standpoint too." [36] This thought was so much on his mind that he wrote Lodge again two days later reiterating it. He said that he had a most friendly feeling for Japan and would do everything he could to help it. Nevertheless, it was a good thing for mankind that the war ended with the Japanese minus an enormous indemnity and still facing Russia in East Asia.[37]

Overall, though Roosevelt did not accurately gauge all the forces at work, the peace conference had been a tremendous success. He had achieved his own principal objective of a balance of power in that the peace treaty confirmed the balance arrived at on the field of battle. Moreover, while securing peace, he had kept the good will of both sides and received a flood of congratulatory messages from heads of state. Even Tsar Nicholas sent his "warmest thanks" to Roosevelt.[38] A fitting tribute to Roosevelt's endeavors came in the next year when Sweden awarded him the Nobel Peace Prize.

---

[35] Roosevelt to Kennan, October 15, 1905, Morison, *Roosevelt Letters, V,* 56–60.

[36] Roosevelt to Lodge, September 6, 1905, Morison, *Roosevelt Letters, V,* 12–13.

[37] Roosevelt to Lodge, September 8, 1905, *Selections from the Correspondence of Theodore Roosevelt and Henry Cabot Lodge, II,* 192.

[38] Tsar Nicholas to Roosevelt, telegram, August 31, 1905, Morison, *Roosevelt Letters, V,* 9.

Britain versus Germany, 1901–1905

3

During Roosevelt's presidency three power rivalries dominated the European diplomatic scene: the Franco-German rivalry, the Austro-Russian rivalry, and the Anglo-German rivalry. Of these, only one commanded Roosevelt's continuing concern, the Anglo-German antagonism. Except for the thirteen-month period of the Moroccan crisis, Britain and Germany were at the center of his view of Europe. The rivalry itself was not always in the forefront of his thoughts, but in his attitude toward European affairs, he almost invariably thought in terms of making a choice between Britain and Germany.

Roosevelt's views towards the Germans and the British are not easily analyzed, for they were ambivalent. He often expressed admiration for the German ruler, William II, but it was a peculiar sort of admiration. He treated the hapless sovereign as immeasurably vain and too dull-witted to see through the most effusive flattery. Similarly he lauded the military splendor and vigor of the German nation, but he believed fundamentally that the Bismarckian attitude toward war was something civilized nations should outgrow. The British he often described as flabby and suffering from the spirit of mere materialism, yet he recognized and valued their close kinship with Americans. He often spoke in uncomplimentary terms about British leaders. But how much of this criticism was sincere is difficult to judge, for he sometimes deliberately feigned an anti-British tone merely to please the Germans. More important than all of these personal manifestations of preference or dislike, however, was one fundamental consideration that dominated his attitudes and policies in world politics: his conviction that Britain was a friend and Germany was a potential enemy.

In the years preceding his ascent to the Presidency, Roosevelt's private correspondence contained many allusions to both the German menace and the British friendship. Typical of these letters was one to Senator Lodge in March 1901, which declared that the United States should be exceedingly cautious about getting embroiled with England, from whom it had "not the least particle of danger to fear in any way or shape." He went on to observe that the only power which was a menace to the United States in the immediate future was Germany.[1] While viewing Germany as a threat, Roosevelt consistently looked upon Britain as America's closest friend. In a letter to William Archer in 1899, he stated that the English-speaking peoples came nearer to one another in ideals, morality, and government than any one of them did to any other peoples. He wished the Germans well where they did not conflict with Britain or the United States, but he hoped there would not be the slightest rift between the English-speaking peoples.[2] Two years later he told Lodge that he was peculiarly anxious to keep on friendly relations with Germany, but he thought the United States closer in feeling to England than to any other power.[3]

British leaders were not altogether happy when Roosevelt entered the White House in 1901, for neither then nor later did they fully understand his pro-British inclinations. In Anglo-American disputes, such as those over an isthmian canal and the Alaskan boundary, the Rough Rider was so pugnaciously pro-American that he appeared to

---

[1] Roosevelt to Lodge, March 27, 1901, Elting E. Morison (ed.), *The Letters of Theodore Roosevelt,* 8 vols. (Cambridge, Mass.: Harvard University Press, 1951–1954), *III,* 32. See also Roosevelt to Francis C. Moore, February 5, 1898; Roosevelt to Captain William K. Kimball, January 9, 1900; and Roosevelt to Meyer, April 12, 1901, Morison, *Roosevelt Letters, I,* 768–769; *II,* 1130; and *III,* 52.

[2] Roosevelt to Archer, August 31, 1899, Morison, *Roosevelt Letters, II,* 1064.

[3] Roosevelt to Lodge, June 19, 1901, Morison, *Roosevelt Letters, III,* 97–98.

them strongly anti-British. What British leaders did not comprehend, however, was that in any Anglo-*German* dispute he could be counted upon to be strongly pro-British. This Lord Lansdowne and others could never quite grasp. Even when Roosevelt left the White House in 1909, after years of siding with Britain in every conflict of interest between that country and Germany, the British only dimly perceived his partiality toward them.

During the Venezuelan crisis in the winter of 1902–1903, Roosevelt's suspicions of Germany and preferences for Britain were apparent. When Britain and Germany momentarily forsook their own antagonism and cooperated to compel Venezuela to pay outstanding claims, American concern and Roosevelt's own ire was directed almost exclusively at Germany. A United States Navy memorandum drafted to guide the Administration during the crisis avoided all references to Britain. It recommended that the United States keep a force at Puerto Rico equal or superior to the German squadron off Venezuela,[4] and this policy Roosevelt followed. While Germany and Britain were blockading Venezuela, Admiral George Dewey, in command of a large fleet, was stationed at Puerto Rico with orders to be ready to advance at a moment's notice. Roosevelt apparently even went so far as to threaten the Germans with dispatching the fleet to the Venezuelan coast. Although his own later recollection of this episode was probably not accurate, it is evident from the German records that he warned Sternburg in February 1903 that he wanted Germany to liquidate its intervention in Venezuela promptly and that the United States fleet at Puerto Rico had secret orders to stand ready for action.[5]

Britain inevitably incurred some American resentment because of

---

[4] Navy memorandum, November, 1902, A. L. P. Dennis, *Adventures in American Diplomacy, 1896–1906* (New York: E. P. Dutton & Co., 1928), pp. 291–292.

[5] Sternburg to the Foreign Office, telegram, February 3, 1903, Germany, Auswärtiges Amt, *Die Grosse Politik der Europäischen Kabinette, 1871–1914*, 40 vols. (Berlin: Deutsche verlagsgesellschaft für politik und geschichte, 1922–1927), *XVII*, 285–286. A full discussion of Roosevelt and the Venezuelan crisis is given in Howard K. Beale, *Theodore Roosevelt and the Rise of America to World Power* (Baltimore: Johns Hopkins Press, 1956), pp. 143–146, 395–432.

its cooperation with Germany. The British Ambassador, Sir Michael Herbert, reported to Foreign Secretary Lansdowne at the height of the crisis: "The impression prevails in Washington that Germany is using us, and our friends here regret, from the point of view of American good feeling towards us, that we are acting with her." [6] The overall effect of the episode was nevertheless an improvement in Anglo-American relations. When the British cabinet realized how unpopular was its cooperation with Germany, both at home and in America, it endeavored to liberate itself from the German connection and bent all efforts toward securing a negotiated settlement of the Venezuelan controversy. Once this was done, Americans were satisfied; more than that, they were pleased that Britain had made solemn obeisance before the Monroe Doctrine. On the British side the episode was equally salutary. The joining of hands with Germany was only a temporary aberration; it could not obscure the growing estrangement between the two nations. As the historian Lionel M. Gelber has observed, when Britain turned away from the New World to face whatever might arise across the North Sea, she viewed it to be in her interest that against the possibility of an *imperium Germanicum* in the Caribbean there should be set up the *pax Americana.*[7]

The Anglo-American friendship that was manifested during the diplomacy of the Venezuelan crisis, was not so apparent during the Russo-Japanese War. Roosevelt sought so earnestly to work in cooperation with the Kaiser that his actions appeared to indicate unusual intimacy between Washington and Berlin. Such an impression was nevertheless misleading. The reason Roosevelt sought the Kaiser's cooperation was that he viewed Germany as the most likely mischief-maker in the Far East. He wished to prevent Japan from being robbed of the fruits of victory and to secure a balance of power in East Asia. British cooperation in this regard he took for granted.

---

[6] Herbert to Lansdowne, December 16, 1902, G. P. Gooch and Harold Temperley, *British Documents on the Origins of the War, 1898–1914,* 11 vols. (London: His Majesty's Stationery Office, 1926–1938), *II,* 162.

[7] Lionel Morris Gelber, *The Rise of Anglo-American Friendship: A Study in World Politics, 1898–1906* (Hamden, Connecticut: Archon Books, 1966, first published 1938), pp. 128, 131.

German cooperation, at the same time, was doubtful. Roosevelt's ardent wooing of the German ruler, therefore, was a courtship born, not of love, but of distrust. Moreover, the Moroccan crisis, which overlapped the Russo-Japanese War in point of time, was destined to reinforce Roosevelt's anti-German attitude. The good will the Kaiser won by his cooperation with Roosevelt in the diplomacy of the Russo-Japanese War was more than counterbalanced by the impact of the Moroccan controversy.

The broad trend of Roosevelt's attitude toward the Kaiser was one of increasing disenchantment, but there were short periods when United States-German friendship appeared to be genuine. The Russo-Japanese War opened on a note of cooperation as both Roosevelt and the Kaiser sought to preserve China's neutrality. The German ruler proposed that Roosevelt take the initiative in urging the belligerents to respect China's neutrality outside the war zone. Roosevelt took up the project and carried it to a successful conclusion, with both the neutral powers and the belligerents falling into line.[8] During the episode, however, Roosevelt became irritated at the British for what he thought to be an uncooperative attitude. The misunderstanding arose because Roosevelt and Hay, in formulating the proposal, expected Manchuria and Korea to be the seat of war, but they did not wish to say so specifically. Instead, they proposed merely that the belligerents "respect the neutrality of China and in all practicable ways her administrative entity." Foreign Secretary Lansdowne deluged Washington with telegrams wanting to know the extent of the neutral territory. Roosevelt and Hay continued to send vague replies to London and marvelled at the British inability to perceive that precision might prevent gaining the general assent of the powers.[9] When it was over, Roosevelt wrote to Root:[10]

As a matter of fact, in this instance Germany behaved better than any other power, for in England Lansdowne drove us half crazy

---

[8] Raymond A. Esthus, *Theodore Roosevelt and Japan* (Seattle, Wash.: University of Washington Press, 1966), pp. 24–34.

[9] Hay diary, February 13, 1904, John Hay Papers, Library of Congress, Washington, D. C.

[10] Roosevelt to Root, February 16, 1904, Morison, *Roosevelt Letters, IV,* 730–732.

with thick-headed inquiries and requests about our making more specific exactly what it was highly inexpedient to make specific at all.

If the incident left Roosevelt with the impression that British and American policies were not moving along parallel lines — and he did seem momentarily to suspect this — he was wrong. Roosevelt always had difficulty in dealing with Lansdowne, but this did not result usually from a difference in policy but from Lansdowne's reluctance to accord the young American President the place on the world stage that he was determined — and destined — to occupy. Actually British policy was in tune with Roosevelt's efforts on China's behalf. Prime Minister Arthur Balfour even contemplated an Anglo-American alliance to protect China's integrity,[11] an idea that he was to revive in 1905.

One reason that the Roosevelt-Lansdowne relationship was lacking in cordiality was that the Foreign Secretary, unlike many of his colleagues, attached no extraordinary importance to the friendship of the United States. This, in turn, was due largely to his belief that Germany was not as dangerous to Britain as other British leaders believed. While Lansdowne was Foreign Secretary, there was a steady rise to power within the Foreign Office of men, such as Sir Frank Bertie and Sir Charles Hardinge, who viewed the rise of German naval power with alarm, but Lansdowne himself was inclined to look at the German problem as just an additional complication of his Russian difficulties. George Monger, who made the first thorough study of British foreign policy from the British records of 1900–1907, says of the Foreign Secretary: "Lansdowne never really understood the most important event in his period of office, the event for which it is now remembered — the estrangement from Germany." [12]

Roosevelt's friend Spring Rice was among those, like Bertie and Hardinge, who took a serious view of the German danger. In a letter to Roosevelt in February 1904, he said that there were many signs in

---

[11] Balfour to Lansdowne, February 11, 1904, Arthur James Balfour Papers, add. mss. 49728, British Museum, London, England; George Monger, *The End of Isolation: British Foreign Policy, 1900–1907* (London and New York: Thomas Nelson & Sons, 1963), p. 155.

[12] Monger, *The End of Isolation,* p. 234.

Germany that an attack on England was being prepared and that it would be immensely popular among the German people. He believed that Germany would seek a combination with Russia, that Russia would embroil England in the war in the Far East, and that Germany would thereupon attack England in Europe. "Germany has for years been preparing popular opinion at home for a war with England," he told Roosevelt. "It is really her only true policy if she is to extend, and she must extend." [13] Roosevelt thought these views overly pessimistic and sought to reassure Springy. He replied that he did not believe there would be a continental coalition against England. He did concede, however, that England was in some immediate danger, as America was in some remote danger, because each was unmilitary when judged by the standards of continental Europe and each suffered from the rottenness of materialism.[14]

Roosevelt attempted to discover from Sternburg whether there was any justification for Spring Rice's fear of a continental coalition against England. After contacting Berlin, Specky assured Roosevelt that there was no truth to "the matter which is worrying Springy so much." [15] Roosevelt apparently accepted this denial at face value, but he would have been wiser to view it with skepticism. Actually, Spring Rice was not so wide of the mark. The Kaiser had for years dreamed of just such a combination against England, and later in 1904 and again in 1905 he would make strenuous efforts to build that coalition. His task was rendered exceedingly difficult in April 1904, however, when England and France signed the Entente Cordiale. Though that agreement did not have, at the outset, the strong anti-German complexion which the Moroccan crisis would soon impart to it, it nevertheless cut across the German ruler's scheme for a continental coalition.

Roosevelt at this time was not greatly worried about the German danger in Europe, but he was alarmed about possible German mis-

---

[13] Stephen Gwynn, *The Letters and Friendships of Sir Cecil Spring Rice: A Record,* 2 vols. (New York and Boston: Houghton Mifflin Co., 1929), *I,* 395–396.

[14] Roosevelt to Spring Rice, March 19, 1904, Morison, *Roosevelt Letters, IV,* 759–761.

[15] Sternburg to Roosevelt, March 24, 1904, Theodore Roosevelt Papers, Library of Congress, Washington, D. C.

chief in the Far East. From talks with Japanese diplomats Roosevelt and Hay learned that Japan was deeply concerned about German interference in the war or in peacemaking.[16] It was this circumstance that precipitated Roosevelt's courtship of the Kaiser in the summer of 1904. Through Sternburg he sought to come to a clear understanding on all East Asiatic questions, and in order to entice Berlin into cooperating with him he suggested that the Chinese viceroy for postwar Manchuria be "appointed by Germany, *not* England." [17]

Chancellor Bernhard von Bülow and Kaiser William liked the anti-British tone Roosevelt took in his talk with Sternburg, but they correctly discerned that he was trying to tie their hands on future action. "The President," said Bülow to the Kaiser, "is a great admirer of Your Majesty and would like to rule the world in hand with Your Majesty, regarding himself as something in the nature of an American counterpart to Your Majesty." Regarding Roosevelt's attempt to pin them down on peace terms for the Russo-Japanese War, the Kaiser noted in the margin of Bülow's report, "One must not divide the hide of the bear before he has been shot." [18] Berlin's official response to Roosevelt's overture was an innocuous statement expressing little more than a desire to maintain the closest possible touch with the President.[19]

While Roosevelt had been ardently attempting to protect Japan from German interference, the Germans had been trying with equal vigor to excite Roosevelt's anxiety over British designs on China's Yangtze valley. It is doubtful that Roosevelt had any serious concern over the danger of British seizure of territory in China, but in the attempt to win the Kaiser's confidence and tie Germany's hands on Far Eastern matters, he at least pretended to lend a sympathetic ear to the German suspicions. If Sternburg's report may be believed, he also

---

[16] Hay to Roosevelt, July 15, 1904, Hay Papers.

[17] Hay diary, August 10, 1904, Hay Papers; Bülow to the Kaiser, August 31, 1904, *Die Grosse Politik, XIX,* 535–537.

[18] Bülow to the Kaiser, August 31, 1904, *Die Grosse Politik, XIX,* 535–537.

[19] Bülow to Sternburg, September 5, 1904, *Die Grosse Politik, XIX,* 541. Roosevelt thought, but without justification, that he had a German pledge not to interfere with the results of the war. Takahira to Komura, October 8, 1904, Telegram Series, *LVI,* 19918–20, Japanese Ministry of Foreign Affairs Archives, microfilm collection, Library of Congress, Washington, D. C.

made uncomplimentary remarks about the British in order to ingratiate himself with the Kaiser. Sternburg reported that in a conversation of September 26 Roosevelt criticized Lansdowne and said that Colonial Secretary Joseph Chamberlain was unreliable and "might jump into the Yangtze valley at any moment." According to Sternburg, Roosevelt exclaimed: "The only man I understand and who understands me is the Kaiser." [20]

Not long after Roosevelt's triumphant reelection in November 1904, the Germans became so encouraged by Sternburg's reports that they actually proposed an alliance directed against the alleged British designs on the Yangtze valley. Roosevelt rebuffed the proposal with excuses about such a treaty having to be submitted to the Senate, which presumably would not approve it;[21] but apart from any constitutional difficulties, it is inconceivable that he would have gone forward with such a project. However much he wished to go hand-in-hand with Germany in the Far East to protect Britain's ally, Japan, he certainly had no desire to join Germany in an alliance directed at Britain.

In late 1904, while Roosevelt was preoccupied with German-Japanese and Anglo-German tensions in the Far East, the Anglo-German rivalry in Europe increased markedly. In September and October reports began to reach the British Foreign Office of Germany's overtures to Russia for an anti-English continental coalition. The rumors appeared to be more solidly based than those which had circulated earlier in the year, and many British leaders believed them.[22] The rumors were indeed well-founded, for the Kaiser was trying desperately to get his cousin "Nicky" to sign an alliance that would make France a junior partner in a grand German-Russian-French combination. When the Russian Baltic fleet fired on some British fishing boats in October 1904 (mistaking them for Japanese torpedo boats), the Tsar was so fearful of war with Britain that he took up the alliance project

---

[20] Sternburg to the Foreign Office, telegram, September 27, 1904, *Die Grosse Politik, XIX,* 541–542.

[21] Sternburg to the Foreign Office, November 17, 1904, *Die Grosse Politik, XIX,* 546–547.

[22] Monger, *The End of Isolation,* p. 165.

with the Kaiser; but once he resolved the dispute with Britain by submitting it to a commission at The Hague, he abandoned the alliance project completely.

The rumors of the Kaiser's activities helped inflame the anti-German feeling in Britain, which reached a peak at the end of 1904. Articles in *Vanity Fair* and the *Army and Navy Journal* hinted that Britain should initiate preventive action against the German fleet. Shortly thereafter the British Navy was reorganized with its strength concentrated in the North Sea.[23] There was a brief period of panic in Germany when a British attack was believed to be imminent. Many Britons believed, at the same time, that Germany intended to attack. Both sides indulged in recriminations, and a feeling of suspicion settled upon both countries. Austen Chamberlain exclaimed in a Foreign Office memorandum that the German Navy was a standing menace to Britain. He went on to chide the German government for remaining silent when the German press daily attacked all things English with a vehemence and scurrility which had no parallel even in Britain's least important journals. Suspicion on the German side was heightened when on February 3, 1905, Roosevelt's friend Arthur Lee, who was Civil Lord of the Admiralty, made a speech in which he dwelt on the power of the British navy to meet and perhaps anticipate an attack from whatever quarter it might come.[24]

Roosevelt viewed the Anglo-German war scare with disgust. He did not believe that either side intended to attack the other, and he blamed both countries for causing the antagonism. In a talk with Sternburg he expressed regret at the bitter animosity between the two countries and criticized the Germans for their tasteless verbal attacks on the British during the Boer War. He also observed to Speck that the British appeared to have lost much of their old self-confidence.[25] While blaming Germany for its past attitude toward Britain, Roosevelt believed that Britain was primarily responsible for precipitating the war scare. In a letter to his British friend John St. Loe

---

[23] E. Llewellyn Woodward, *Great Britain and the German Navy* (Oxford: The Clarendon Press, 1935), pp. 84–85.

[24] Monger, *The End of Isolation,* pp. 175–177.

[25] Sternburg to Bülow, February 10, 1905, *Die Grosse Politik, XIX,* 570–575.

Strachey some years later, he ascribed the crisis to the "very foolish and irresponsible talk in England." [26]

As Anglo-German tension mounted, Roosevelt moved to establish closer cooperation with Britain. Since he found it difficult to work on close terms with Ambassador Durand, he sought to open other channels. First he arranged through Bob Ferguson, a friend of Spring Rice who was in the United States, to have a member of the London *Times* staff visit Washington. In November 1904, Sir Valentine Chirol crossed the ocean to confer with Roosevelt and other American leaders, at which time he was told of the desire of the United States to work closely with the British.[27] The Chirol visit turned out to be only the beginning of Roosevelt's endeavors to establish closer alignment with Whitehall. Soon after Chirol left the American capital, Roosevelt dispatched a long letter to Spring Rice setting forth his thoughts on developments in the Russo-Japanese War and inviting him to come to Washington for a talk so that Springy could, as Roosevelt put it, "tell your people just what I think of things." [28] Spring Rice was on leave in London at this time, and Roosevelt sent the letter through Henry White, who was Secretary at the Embassy in London. In a covering letter he asked White to help make the necessary arrangements with the Foreign Office. He confided to White that he did not have much faith in the British tenacity of purpose, nor did he know what position the American people would be willing to take, but he wanted at least to get a clear idea of the respective mental attitudes of the two governments.[29]

The Foreign Office was loath to send Spring Rice for fear of giving offense to Ambassador Durand, but it was arranged that he devote part of his leave to a "private" visit to Washington. Roosevelt was delighted. He requested Hay to ask Henry Adams if he could lodge

---

[26] Roosevelt to Strachey, February 22, 1907, Morison, *Roosevelt Letters, V,* 596–598.

[27] Chirol to Spring Rice, November 1 and 15, 1904, Chirol to Florence Spring Rice, December 2 and 14, 1904, Spring Rice to Chirol, November 7, 1904, Spring Rice Papers, custody of Lady Elizabeth Arthur, London, England.

[28] Roosevelt to Spring Rice, December 27, 1904, Morison, *Roosevelt Letters, IV,* 1082–1088.

[29] Roosevelt to White, December 27, 1904, Morison, *Roosevelt Letters, IV,* 1082.

"this distinguished member of the kitchen ambassadorial circle." [30] That Lansdowne did not share the President's enthusiasm for the project, at least at the outset, was apparent in remarks he made to White. He cautioned that it would be difficult for Spring Rice to express any opinion as to policy in the Far East and that Britain had no active policy in view. White gained the impression that Lansdowne was waiting to see what would happen in East Asia and what the United States was willing to do.[31]

However hesitant the Foreign Office may have been to have this unofficial contact with the American President, Prime Minister Balfour welcomed it. At this time he was pondering the question of renewing the alliance with Japan. He had little enthusiasm for the alliance as then constituted, preferring instead a triple alliance which included the United States and which guaranteed China's integrity. "If we could bring in the Americans," he wrote to Under Secretary Earl Percy, "that would be a new arrangement, and, as part of it, an extension of the Japanese Treaty would clearly be legitimate." [32] Thus, while it was Roosevelt who took the initiative for close diplomatic cooperation with Britain, Balfour was thinking of an even closer arrangement than that contemplated by Roosevelt.

When Lansdowne informed Balfour that Spring Rice was going to Washington, the Prime Minister drafted a letter to Spring Rice setting forth a proposal for an Anglo-American alliance. If America and Britain joined together in a treaty to resist an attack on China's integrity, he asserted, no such aggression would be attempted, for together those two countries were too strong for any combination of powers to oppose. Balfour thought there would be no obstacle on his side of the Atlantic in the way of such a treaty. "The difficulty," he believed, "would be rather with the United States, whose traditions and whose constitution conspire to make such arrangements hard to conclude." [33] Balfour's assessment of the prospects for

---

[30] Roosevelt to Hay, January 13, 1905, Morison, *Roosevelt Letters, IV,* 1102.

[31] White to Roosevelt, January 13, 1905, Roosevelt Papers.

[32] Balfour to Percy, January 15, 1905, Balfour Papers, add. mss. 49747; Monger, *The End of Isolation,* p. 180.

[33] Draft letter, Balfour to Spring Rice, January 17, 1905, Balfour Papers, add. mss. 49729. Later in the year Balfour noted in a letter to Ambassador Choate

such a treaty was, of course, accurate, and he decided not to send the letter to Spring Rice. It is likely, nevertheless, that Lansdowne saw the draft before Spring Rice left London and gave him at least a hint of Balfour's alliance idea when he talked with him on January 17.[34] American records reveal that when Spring Rice reached Washington he discussed the question of an alliance with both Hay and Roosevelt.

Before Spring Rice arrived in the American capital, Roosevelt took another step to further Anglo-American cooperation. He was so anxious to achieve a thorough understanding with Britain that he momentarily overcame his distaste for Ambassador Durand and called him to the White House for a long conference. He explained to Durand that events in the Russo-Japanese War might occur quickly and force him to decide upon a line of action. He therefore wished to know Britain's preferences ahead of time as much as possible. Specifically he wished to know whether Britain shared his views on possible peace terms, which he envisaged as including the retention of Port Arthur by Japan, paramount Japanese influence in Korea, and the restoration of Manchuria to China. "England and America must stand together," he declared — and he repeated these words two or three times in what Durand called "his vehement way." Roosevelt expressed himself so forcefully that Durand reported to Lansdowne that he was surprised at the strength of the President's language and its very friendly tone. The frankness of Roosevelt's remarks about Germany must have startled Durand also. He told the Ambassador that he really liked the Emperor but thought him very dangerous. No one in America still thought of England as a possible enemy, he said, but Germany was the chosen foe of the Navy — and not just the

that the conviction that the two co-heirs of Anglo-Saxon freedom shared a common mission had developed more quickly on the British side than on the American. Balfour to Choate, June 1, 1905, Balfour Papers, add. mss. 49742.

[34] Lansdowne sent Balfour detailed comments on the draft on January 18, so it is likely that it was in his possession the day before when he saw Spring Rice. Lansdowne to Balfour, January 18, 1905, Balfour Papers, add. mss. 49729.

Navy. When Durand left the White House, he was convinced that Roosevelt regarded England as America's best friend.[35]

Lansdowne was gratified at Roosevelt's initiative. On receiving Durand's telegram he commented to Balfour:[36]

> It is satisfactory that Roosevelt has broken the ice with him, for I could not help feeling a little uneasy at the proposed extra-official communications between the President and Spring Rice at a moment when the former was keeping our ambassador at arm's length.

After conferring with Balfour, Lansdowne sent a long telegraphic reply to Roosevelt assuring him that Britain was in general agreement with his views for a peace settlement between Russia and Japan and expressing an earnest desire to remain in line with the United States.[37] The Foreign Secretary also sent a private letter to Durand authorizing him to tell Roosevelt that King Edward had seen Durand's reports and was much pleased at the President's language.[38]

Meanwhile Spring Rice journeyed to Washington where he arrived in late January 1905. Soon after his arrival he was closeted in long discussions with Roosevelt and Hay. Durand was brought into the talks on occasion, and Roosevelt also conferred separately with the Ambassador while the pourparlers with Spring Rice went on. Roosevelt told Spring Rice bluntly at the outset that an alliance was impossible and the less said about it the better. Nevertheless, in the

---

[35] Durand to Lansdowne, telegram, January 23, 1905, and letter January 26, 1905, Lansdowne Papers, F. O. 800/116, Public Record Office, London, England.

[36] Lansdowne to Balfour, January 23, 1905, Balfour Papers, add. mss. 49729.

[37] Lansdowne to Durand, telegram, January 25, 1905, Lansdowne Papers, F. O. 800/144. Regarding Russian annexation of part of Manchuria, Lansdowne's telegram indicated that he was not entirely "in line" with the United States. Whereas in his conversation with Durand on December 22 Roosevelt had spoken with a feeling of resignation about the fact that the American public would not support a war to prevent Russian annexation of Chinese territory, Lansdowne expressed the thought that all nations concerned, including China and Japan, might favor some cession of Manchurian territory to Russia. This view was probably Lansdowne's alone, though, for Balfour constantly reiterated a desire to protect China's integrity.

[38] Lansdowne to Durand, February 4, 1905, Lansdowne Papers, F. 0. 800/144.

Far East Anglo-American interests were identical and there should be no difficulty about parallel action. Spring Rice said that his government understood "as a matter of course" that the United States could not make a treaty but that Britain also was ready to do everything that could be done in the way of concurrent action.[39] As the talks progressed, Durand brought assurances from Lansdowne that he wished to walk shoulder-to-shoulder with the United States and that Anglo-American interests regarding the open door and the integrity of China were identical.[40] Durand assured Lansdowne in return that Roosevelt was "thoroughly with us." He cautioned the Foreign Secretary, however, that Roosevelt wished the two governments not to excite alarm or criticism by an "open evident agreement." England and America must stand together but must show they stand together only by their actions.[41] The Senate and the people, said Durand, though no longer unfriendly to England, were suspicious of any entangling alliances and were watchful.[42]

From these talks in late January and early February of 1905 no specific guidelines for Anglo-American diplomatic cooperation emerged. British and American policies, insofar as they existed, were already running roughly in parallel lines before the talks, and they continued in the same paths afterwards. As Spring Rice described matters to Chirol after his return to England: "To sum up — no treaty, no convention, no understanding of a concrete kind — but a general community of interests and communion of ideas. The two vessels sail on parallel courses and should have a common code of signals." [43]

Meanwhile Roosevelt had responded to another diplomatic initiative from Berlin. In January 1905, the German Emperor sent to Roosevelt another warning that England planned to seize the Yangtze valley. This time he alleged that a coalition led by Britain and France

---

[39] Hay diary, January 30 and February 2, 1905, Hay Papers; Memoranda by Spring Rice, February, 1905, Lansdowne Papers, F. O. 800/116.

[40] Hay diary, February 2, 1905, Hay Papers.

[41] Durand to Lansdowne, telegram, January 30, 1905, Lansdowne Papers, F. O. 800/116.

[42] Durand to Lansdowne, February 6, 1905, Lansdowne Papers, F. O. 800/116.

[43] Spring Rice to Chirol, March 26, 1905, Spring Rice Papers, custody of Lady Elizabeth Arthur, London, England.

intended to intervene to bring peace in the Russo-Japanese War and in the process seize Chinese territory. He suggested that Roosevelt ask the neutral powers to pledge that they would not demand territorial compensation in China.[44] Roosevelt told Sternburg that he would be astonished if England really intended to do as the Kaiser thought likely,[45] but he nevertheless decided to take up the Kaiser's proposal. In doing so he was probably more anxious to pin Germany down than to get Britain's pledge. Hay noted in his diary on January 9, after conferring with the President:[46]

> I found him full of the proposition of the German Emperor. He had come to the same conclusion at which I had arrived the day before: that it would be best to take advantage of the Kaiser's proposition, 1st. to nail the matter with him and 2nd. to ascertain the views of the other powers.

Hay dispatched the requests to the neutral powers on January 13, and within a short time all gave reasonably satisfactory pledges. Although Hay did not seek similar pledges from Japan and Russia, the support which the neutrals pledged for China's integrity obviously made it more difficult for the belligerents to annex Chinese territory. The Russian newspaper *Novosti* commented on the episode: "We cannot say that it promises the belligerents agreeable prospects." [47]

The visit of Spring Rice and the outcome of the démarche in support of China's integrity made Roosevelt less apprehensive about developments in the Far East. Meanwhile the fall of Port Arthur to Japanese forces in January 1905 appeared to indicate that Japan would continue to be successful on the field of battle. In view of these developments, the fear of German mischief-making in the Far East noticeably receded. As the German menace declined, so did Roosevelt's interest in cultivating the German Emperor's friendship. The year 1905 would not see frantic wooing of the German ruler by

---

[44] Sternburg to Roosevelt, January 5, 1905, Roosevelt Papers.
[45] Roosevelt to Sternburg, January 12, 1905, Morison, *Roosevelt Letters, IV,* 1100–1101.
[46] Hay diary, January 9, 1905, Hay Papers.
[47] Hay to Roosevelt, January 31, 1905, Hay Papers.

the American President such as had occurred in 1904. Instead it would witness a continuing endeavor to work closely with Britain.

It was Britain, in the person of King Edward VII, that took the next initiative for closer Anglo-American ties. The King viewed the German danger to British security more seriously than Lansdowne, and he believed that in the context of the developing Anglo-German rivalry Roosevelt's friendship was worth cultivating. His first step was to send a message to Roosevelt through Henry White, who was going on leave to the United States. The communication was candid, to say the least. The King expressed the hope that Roosevelt would never allow himself to be persuaded by any other sovereign or government that they could be as good a friend to the United States as Great Britain.[48] When White delivered this message, Roosevelt knew to which sovereign and country King Edward referred. He knew also that the King stated the case correctly, but he was amused. He wrote to Hay: "Uncle Edward evidently has his eye on Nephew William, and sings a variant on the old song that 'Codlin is our friend and not Short.' "[49]

King Edward took the occasion of Roosevelt's second inauguration to continue his cultivation of Roosevelt's friendship. He drafted a letter of congratulation to the President which was so effusive that government leaders felt it best to tone it down. Even then it was a cordial, personal communication.[50] The King also selected a gift to accompany the letter. With the aid of Spring Rice he chose a miniature of John Hampden, a seventeenth century Puritan leader, and dispatched it to Roosevelt over the strong objections of his librarian at Windsor, who thought it too valuable to part with.[51] Spring Rice confided to Hay that the King was so eager in taking the lead with Roosevelt that his enthusiasm had to be "damped with constitutional

---

[48] White to Roosevelt, February 25, 1905, Roosevelt Papers; Gwynn, *Letters and Friendships of Sir Cecil Spring Rice, I,* 451.

[49] Roosevelt to Hay, February 27, 1905, Morison, *Roosevelt Letters, IV,* 1128.

[50] Sir Sidney Lee, *Edward VII, A Biography,* 2 vols. (New York: The Macmillan Co., 1925–1927), *II,* 429–431.

[51] Spring Rice to Roosevelt, May 7, 1910, Gwynn, *Letters and Friendships of Sir Cecil Spring Rice, I,* 452.

reminders." [52]   When Durand presented the letter and gift on the
eve of the inauguration, Roosevelt was genuinely impressed. He
spoke warmly about the tone of the letter which, he told Durand,
differed in that respect from any that he had ever received from a
crowned head. He went on to tell Durand:[53]

> I know 'Springy' thinks I am inclined to fall under the influence
> of the German Emperor, but he is quite wrong. I like the Em-
> peror very much in a way, but I don't trust him and am not in the
> least affected by the ridiculous messages he makes 'Specky'
> bring me. . . . You need never be the least afraid that I shall
> take the Kaiser seriously.

After the inauguration Roosevelt sent a reply to King Edward stating
that he agreed with him absolutely as to the importance of a constantly growing friendship and understanding between the English-
speaking peoples.[54]

The same month that Roosevelt was inaugurated, March of 1905,
an event occurred which caused Roosevelt's regard for the Kaiser to
decline sharply: the German ruler's dramatic visit to Tangier, openly
challenging France's ascendancy in Morocco and its newly made
Entente Cordiale with England. As the Moroccan question escalated
into a major world crisis, Roosevelt went out of his way to assure
his friends and associates that he was not under the Kaiser's influence.
To Spring Rice he wrote: "Of course in a way I suppose it is natural
that my English friends generally, from the King down, should think
I was under the influence of the Kaiser, but you ought to know better,
old man." He went on to assure Springy that he could not follow or
take too seriously "a man whose policy is one of such violent and
often irrational zigzags." [55] To Ambassador Jusserand he remarked

---

[52] Spring Rice to Hay, March 15, 1905, Gwynn, *Letters and Friendships of Sir
Cecil Spring Rice, I,* 462.

[53] Durand to Lansdowne, March 10, 1905, Lansdowne Papers, F.O. 800/144;
Gwynn, *Letters and Friendships of Sir Cecil Spring Rice, I,* 453–455; Sir
Percy M. Sykes, *The Right Honourable Sir Mortimer Durand* (London: Cassell
& Co., Ltd., 1926), pp. 279–281.

[54] Roosevelt to Edward VII, March 9, 1905, Morison, *Roosevelt Letters, IV,*
1135–1136.

[55] Roosevelt to Spring Rice, May 13, 1905, Morison, *Roosevelt Letters, IV,*
1177–1179.

that he had had an inclination for the Kaiser for a year or two but nothing was left of that — it was passed, adjudicated.[56] To Lodge he wrote:[57]

> It always amuses me to find that the English think I am under the influence of the Kaiser. The heavy witted creatures do not understand that nothing would persuade me to follow the lead of or enter into close alliance with a man who is so jumpy. . . .

Lodge agreed and added that the German ruler was easily understood — unstable, crazy for notoriety, and not to be trusted.[58]

At this time Lodge was planning a trip to Europe, later in the year, and Roosevelt seized the opportunity to give further reassurance to the British. He instructed Lodge:[59]

> When you see King Edward, explain my very real pleasure that we are able to work together in the Far East. Also say I appreciate thoroughly that in the long run the English people are more apt to be friendly to us than any other.

In another letter to Lodge he instructed him to tell the King exactly his relations with the Kaiser; to wit, that he intended to keep relations with Germany on a good footing but that it was "a simple wild nightmare to suppose that he can use me to the detriment of any other nation." [60]

The developing Moroccan crisis focused Roosevelt's attention increasingly on the Anglo-German rivalry. Before leaving on a hunting trip in the West in April, he talked with Ambassador Durand and attempted to reassure him regarding German intentions. Durand insisted that Germany was planning war against England, whereupon Roosevelt exclaimed, "I am giving you a pledge that Germany has no

---

[56] Jean Jules Jusserand, *What Me Befell: The Reminiscences of J. J. Jusserand* (Boston and New York: Houghton Mifflin Co., 1933), p. 267.

[57] Roosevelt to Lodge, May 15, 1905, Morison, *Roosevelt Letters, IV*, 1181.

[58] Lodge to Roosevelt, June 3, 1905, *Selections from the Correspondence of Theodore Roosevelt and Henry Cabot Lodge, 1884–1918*, 2 vols. (New York: Charles Scribner's Sons, 1925), *II*, 128.

[59] Roosevelt to Lodge, May 24 ,1905, Morison, *Roosevelt Letters, IV*, 1192–1193.

[60] Roosevelt to Lodge, June 16, 1905, Morison, *Roosevelt Letters, IV*, 1221.

such intentions." When Durand inquired as to whose pledge Roosevelt was giving, the President said, "Sternburg's word." [61] Durand doubtless remained unpersuaded.

After Roosevelt left Washington for the West, he was drawn directly into the Anglo-German question by entreaties from Berlin. The German government was anxious for Roosevelt to use his influence with the British to detach them from supporting France in the Moroccan dispute. Roosevelt was reluctant to get involved in the Franco-German rivalry, but he did wish to improve Anglo-German relations. He wrote Taft, who had been left in Washington to "sit on the lid," that he did not care to take sides between France and Germany but that he was sincerely anxious to bring about a better state of feeling between England and Germany. He went on to tell Taft that each country was working itself up to a condition of desperate hatred of the other, that the Kaiser was dead sure that England intended to attack him and the English were equally sure that Germany intended to attack England.[62]

On Roosevelt's instructions Taft conferred with Durand to sound him on British policy. He explained that the President's action in the matter grew out of a real concern that through sheer misunderstanding England and Germany might be brought into a feeling of hostility. Durand agreed to relay the President's views to London, but his comments to Taft did not give promise that Roosevelt's initiative would be successful in improving Anglo-German relations. The Ambassador said that his government distrusted Germany because it had good reason to, that the German government had played tricks with the English for many years. It would be very difficult, he said, to induce Englishmen to believe that Germany was sincere in its expressed desire for friendship. He went on to observe that he frankly could not account for the enmity which the German government and people seemed to cherish towards England.[63]

---

[61] Sternburg to the Foreign Office, April 1, 1905, *Die Grosse Politik, XIX,* 590–591.

[62] Roosevelt to Taft, April 20, 1905, Morison, *Roosevelt Letters, IV,* 1161–1162.

[63] Taft to Roosevelt, April 26, 1905, Roosevelt Papers; Durand to Lansdowne, April 26, 1905, *British Documents, III,* 67–68.

Foreign Secretary Lansdowne gave a cool rebuff to Roosevelt. He instructed Durand that he might reassure the President that there was no subject of dispute between England and Germany or any reason why their relations should not be of a friendly description, and he told Durand to say nothing which could be interpreted as an invitation to Roosevelt to act as mediator between England and Germany.[64] Lansdowne sent this curt message without consulting Balfour, and when he informed the Prime Minister he justified his action by observing, "Roosevelt terrifies me almost as much as the German Emperor." [65] Why Lansdowne had so little confidence in Roosevelt is not altogether clear, for only a few months earlier he had declared his resolve to walk shoulder-to-shoulder with him in the Far East. Perhaps Durand's criticisms of Roosevelt were partly responsible for Lansdowne's attitude. In both private letters and official dispatches to London the Ambassador had often commented on Roosevelt's impetuousness. When Hay on one occasion remarked to Durand that he expected to be soon "twanging a golden harp in another country," Durand lamented to Lansdowne:[66]

> I hope he may be wrong for I like him personally, and I feel that the loss of his restraining influence would be a serious thing for us. Roosevelt is impulsive, not to say aggressive, and he was at one time anything but friendly to England.

Spring Rice's visit to Washington early in 1905 had temporarily smoothed things over between Durand and Roosevelt, but by early April Durand was again telling Lansdowne that Roosevelt was unreliable. Hay at this time had gone to Europe in the forlorn hope of regaining his health, and Durand warned Lansdowne that "without Hay to keep him steady there is no saying what he may do." [67] Thus whatever gain Roosevelt had made in winning the confidence of the Foreign Office during Spring Rice's visit had been largely dissipated by the spring of 1905.

---

[64] Lansdowne to Durand, April 27, 1905, *British Documents, III,* 68.

[65] Lansdowne to Balfour, April 27, 1905, Balfour Papers, add. mss. 49729.

[66] Durand to Lansdowne, November 29, 1904, Lansdowne Papers, F. O. 800/144; Sykes, *Durand,* p. 275.

[67] Durand to Lansdowne, April 7, 1905, Lansdowne Papers, F. O. 800/116.

Lansdowne's tactless rejection of Roosevelt's offer to work for a better understanding between London and Berlin was apparently transmitted in undiluted form. What words Durand used in delivering it through Taft is not known, but Roosevelt understood the meaning. After he returned from the hunting trip, he told Sternburg that the British government had made it clear it did not wish better relations with Germany. Taft had been told, he said, that England was able to attend to its own affairs. More, said Roosevelt, he could not do without risking discourtesy.[68] Roosevelt was obviously disgruntled at the British rebuff. He wrote to Ambassador Meyer at St. Petersburg: "It is perfectly hopeless to try to bring about a better understanding between England and Germany. I attempted it in vain." [69]

Lansdowne's attitude was ungracious, to say the least, and — what was worse — unrealistic. Despite Lansdowne's statement to the contrary, there was a specific dispute between England and Germany, the Moroccan dispute, and behind this lay the deeper problem of naval competition. If Lansdowne had perceived even an inkling of the service Roosevelt would render England and France in the Moroccan question, he should have been stumbling over himself in eagerness to bring the American President into the dispute. Happily for England, however much irritation Roosevelt felt, it did not restrain him from becoming involved in the Moroccan muddle. He was soon knee-deep in the controversy. Meanwhile he continued the endeavor to pour oil on the troubled Anglo-German waters. He wrote Spring Rice in May that he did not for one moment believe that the Kaiser had any long-settled and well-thought-out plans for an attack on England. The German ruler, he believed, was altogether too jumpy and too erratic to carry out such a policy.[70]

In his reassuring letters to Spring Rice, Roosevelt repeatedly advanced one argument which was not well founded. He theorized

[68] Sternburg to the Foreign Office, telegram, May 19, 1905, *Die Grosse Politik, XIX*, 603–604.

[69] Roosevelt to Meyer, May 22, 1905, Morison, *Roosevelt Letters, IV,* 1189.

[70] Roosevelt to Spring Rice, May 13, 1905, Morison, *Roosevelt Letters, IV,* 1177–1179. See also Roosevelt to Spring Rice, May 26, 1905, Morison, *Roosevelt Letters, IV,* 1194–1195.

that Germany's bullying of France over the Moroccan issue was positive proof that Germany was not attempting to construct an anti-English continental coalition. It is now known that the Kaiser was, in
fact, seeking to do just that. He had first attempted to do so in the
fall of 1904, and now in the summer of 1905 he redoubled his efforts
to build such a combination. In July at the famous meeting of the
Kaiser and the Tsar at Björkö, he actually achieved a momentary success in getting the Tsar's assent to an alliance. Roosevelt's understanding of the Kaiser's activities would have been more accurate if
the German ruler had had his own way. He was so elated about the
alliance that he wished to send news of it to "his friend" Roosevelt.
It took the combined opposition of Chancellor Bülow and Baron
Friedrich von Holstein to restrain him from confiding in the President.[71] Fortunately for the British, the Tsar found that he could not
change the whole direction of Russian policy with a stroke of the
pen, and the Kaiser's plans for a continental coalition again proved
abortive.

Roosevelt's assessment of the Anglo-German rivalry was probably
inaccurate also with respect to the developing naval competition. In
March 1905 he told Durand that the British attached too much
importance to German naval preparations.[72] This assessment by
Roosevelt hardly squared with a realistic calculation of power rela-
tionships. As long as Britain had overwhelming naval superiority it
could protect itself and yet pose no mortal threat to Germany. England could not hope to match Germany on land, and the British
navy could not get to Berlin. Germany's might on land, at the same
time, posed no mortal threat to Britain, for that army could not cross
the channel. Thus a delicate balance of power existed between
Britain and Germany in which each was powerful in its own way
but could not seriously threaten the existence of the other. But if
Germany built a navy which endangered Britain's overwhelming
superiority in the waters surrounding the British Isles, that balance
would be destroyed, and Britain would be subjected, if not to outright

---

[71] Bülow to the Foreign Office, telegrams (nos. 24 and 25), July 26, 1905,
and Holstein to Bülow, July 26, 1905, *Die Grosse Politik*, XIX, 466–470.
[72] Sykes, *Durand*, pp. 279–281.

attack, at least to constant diplomatic blackmail by the Germans. As Sir Eyre Crowe was to note in his classic analysis in early 1907, it mattered little whether the naval threat resulted from a conscious long-range policy on the part of Germany or from a vague, confused German policy in which the statesmen did not realize its own drift. The danger to Britain would be the same.[73]

When in June 1905 Germany threatened France with war over the Moroccan question, Roosevelt's assessment of the Anglo-German rivalry became more realistic. That development destroyed his confidence that Germany did not contemplate an attack on Britain. He became so alarmed that he sent a direct warning to the Kaiser that if Germany attacked England it would lose all its colonies and the "high and honorable fame" of the Kaiser might be clouded.[74] He then confided his anxieties to the British. He told Durand that a year ago he thought the Emperor nothing more than "inconvenient" in his ways, but he now thought him really dangerous. He went on to recount the warning he had sent to the Kaiser and observed that if Germany developed designs on Holland, the United States would take over Dutch possessions in the Western hemisphere. Durand reported to London:[75]

> I have no doubt the President wished me to know that the Emperor was contemplating the possibility of war with England, but I feel sure he understands that much as we should regret war we are not in the least afraid of it, or in the mood to be bullied.

Early in the following month (August 1905) Roosevelt received further indications of the depth of Anglo-German hostility. Ambassador Tower at Berlin sent him an account of a long talk he recently had with the British Ambassador, Sir Frank Lascelles, who had returned to Berlin after consultations in London. Lascelles had told him that King Edward was intensely irritated by the actions of the Kaiser, whom he suspected of trying to damage England in every part of the world.

---

[73] Memorandum by Sir Eyre Crowe, January 1, 1907, *British Documents, III,* 397–420.

[74] Roosevelt to Sternburg, June 25, 1905, Morison, *Roosevelt Letters, IV,* 1257.

[75] Durand to Lansdowne, June 27, 1905, Lansdowne Papers, F. O. 800/116; Sykes, *Durand,* pp. 287–288.

Lascelles confided to him that he was so depressed that he had told Lansdowne that his mission had been a failure and that a new ambassador should be sent to Berlin. Tower himself believed that the friction between the two countries had greatly increased and that there existed a degree of mutual suspicion that was exceedingly dangerous and might lead to the gravest results.[76]

Spring Rice sent Roosevelt at this time an equally disturbing report. The British, said Springy, had an uncomfortable feeling "that always and everywhere we encounter the fixed and determined hostility of Germany, and that, when opportunity offers, this hostility will take an active form." [77] In a later letter Spring Rice took a calmer tone, expressing the thought that it was out of the question that Germany or England would be guilty of unprovoked aggression;[78] but his letters continued to reflect apprehension over the Anglo-German hostility. Though Roosevelt had previously minimized the German danger, he now made no attempt to send soothing words to his British friend. "I don't know what to say as to the relations you set forth as existing between Germany and England," he wrote on November 1. "I think you are entirely right in your statement of these relations; but I have no idea how to make them better." He did assure Spring Rice, however, that England and the United States, beyond any other two powers, should be friendly with one another.[79]

Spring Rice was doubtless glad to get the President's reassurance regarding Anglo-American friendship, for his government had incurred Roosevelt's displeasure during the recent negotiations ending the Russo-Japanese War. In July and August of 1905 Roosevelt sought the aid of the European powers in his peace efforts, and while the Kaiser gave him full support, Britain repeatedly refused to bring pressure on Japan to make peace. The previous January London had

---

[76] Tower to Roosevelt, August 3, 1905, Despatches: Germany, LXXXIV, Department of State Records, National Archives, Washington, D. C.

[77] Spring Rice to Mrs. Roosevelt, August 10, 1905, Gwynn, Letters and Friendships of Sir Cecil Spring Rice, I, 484.

[78] Spring Rice to Mrs. Roosevelt, October 15, 1905, Gwynn, Letters and Friendships of Sir Cecil Spring Rice, I, 503.

[79] Roosevelt to Spring Rice, November 1, 1905, Morison, Roosevelt Letters, V, 63.

declared its resolve to go hand-in-hand with Washington, but the first time that resolve was put to a test Whitehall demurred. The British, including Spring Rice, were convinced that to urge moderation upon Japan during the peace negotiations would be to break the spirit of the Anglo-Japanese Alliance.[80] Roosevelt disagreed, and he was greatly irritated by the refusal of Britain to urge peace at Tokyo. By the time the negotiations at Portsmouth reached a successful conclusion in September 1905, however, his irritation had subsided. He had been informed that Britain had negotiated a renewal of the Anglo-Japanese Alliance, and he realized that this had aided the cause of peace by giving Japan security for the future. That the episode had not changed his basically pro-British attitude was apparent in a letter he sent to Ambassador Reid on September 11. "I think," he said, "England has a more sincere feeling of friendliness for us than has any other power." [81] Roosevelt's pro-British inclinations were doubtless not harmed by a report Reid sent to him on the same day. At a luncheon with King Edward, reported Reid, the Sovereign had stated that he was "simply lost in admiration" of the President and his work.[82]

The support Roosevelt had secured from Germany for his peace endeavor meanwhile had not changed his attitude towards that nation. He genuinely appreciated William II's aid, but he continued to view him with suspicion and distrust. On October 1, at a family dinner at the White House to which Jusserand was invited, Roosevelt declared that it would be imprudent to count on the Kaiser's most solemn assurances. Jusserand reported to Paris that though Roosevelt continued to show the greatest courtesy, he placed no confidence whatever in the German Emperor.[83]

Roosevelt's leaning toward Britain was further evidenced by his

---

[80] Spring Rice to Lansdowne, July 9, 1905, Lansdowne Papers, F. O. 800/116.
[81] Roosevelt to Reid, September 11, 1905, Morison, *Roosevelt Letters, V,* 18–19.
[82] Reid to Roosevelt, September 11, 1905, Roosevelt Papers.
[83] Jusserand to Rouvier, telegram, October 2, 1905, France, Ministère des Affaires Etrangères, *Documents Diplomatique Francais (1871–1914),* 2nd. series (Paris: Imprimerie Nationale, 1930–1955), 2nd. series, *VIII,* 11–12.

wholehearted approval of the Anglo-Japanese Alliance. In the famous Taft-Katsura conversation of July 27, 1905, Roosevelt's Secretary of War told the Japanese Prime Minister that the United States was so fully in accord with the policy of the Anglo-Japanese Alliance in the maintenance of peace in the Far East that cooperation could be counted on as confidently as if the United States were under treaty obligations. Taft had not made this assertion under instructions, but Roosevelt gave unequivocal endorsement to the statement when informed of it. "Wish you would state to Katsura that I confirm every word you have said," he cabled enthusiastically to Taft.[84] A few days later Roosevelt confided to Ambassador Durand the substance of Taft's statement.[85]

Strangely, Roosevelt had difficulty convincing British leaders of his approval of the Anglo-Japanese Alliance. In October 1905 Lansdowne telegraphed Durand anxiously that Foreign Minister Lamsdorff had told the British Ambassador at St. Petersburg that Roosevelt viewed the Anglo-Japanese Alliance with dissatisfaction and that a Russian-American-German coalition might be formed to counteract the designs of Britain and Japan.[86] Durand assured Lansdowne that he was certain there was no foundation for the report, for the President had spoken with unreserved approval of the Anglo-Japanese Alliance. Durand went on, however, to make comments that were hardly reassuring. Roosevelt, he said, had never entertained any sentimental feeling in favor of England. His cooler judgment had gradually led him to the conviction that American interests were bound up with those of England — at times he had even seemed really friendly — but his prejudices were all in the other direction.[87]

Despite Durand's farfetched theories about Roosevelt's prejudices, British anxieties must have been dispelled by later reports Durand sent to London. In November he telegraphed Lansdowne that

---

[84] Details of the Taft-Katsura conversation may be found in Esthus, "The Taft-Katsura Agreement — Reality or Myth," *Journal of Modern History*, XXXI (1959), pp. 46–51.

[85] Durand to Lansdowne, telegram, August 4, 1905, F. O. 115/1360.

[86] Lansdowne to Durand, telegram, October 19, 1905, F. O. 115/1360.

[87] Durand to Lansdowne, telegram, October 22, 1905, F. O. 115/1360.

Roosevelt had assured him personally that he was and always had been unreservedly in favor of the Anglo-Japanese treaty.[88] In January 1906 Durand sent an even more revealing report to London. He had talked with Roosevelt again and the President had spoken with indignation of the report that he was opposed to the Anglo-Japanese Alliance. More than that, Roosevelt had assured him that England was the one country with which the United States ought to be on terms of close and confidential friendship and so long as he remained at the White House this would be a cardinal principle of his foreign policy.[89] In a private letter to the new Foreign Secretary, Sir Edward Grey, Durand said of his talk with Roosevelt, "I have never known him more friendly and unreserved." [90]

Thus as the year 1906 opened Roosevelt was firmly aligned with the Anglo-Japanese combination in the Far East. Meanwhile the Moroccan dispute had brought a similar attachment to the Anglo-French Entente in Europe.

---

[88] Durand to Lansdowne, telegram, November 6, 1905, F. O. 115/1360.
[89] Durand to Sir Edward Grey, telegram, January 2, 1906, Papers of Sir Edward Grey, F. O. 800/81, Public Record Office, London, England; Sykes, *Durand*, p. 299.
[90] Durand to Grey, January 11, 1906, Grey Papers, F. O. 800/81.

The Moroccan Crisis

4

The Moroccan dispute was the first in the series of crises that convulsed Europe in the decade preceding the First World War. That a bleak land like Morocco should bring the world to the verge of war was indeed strange. Apart from its geographical position astride the entrance from the Atlantic into the Mediterranean Sea, it was a country of little importance. Three-fourths of its area consisted of unsubdued lands, the Blad-el-Siba, and the remaining portion, though under the sway of a young sultan who was fascinated with things European, was largely untouched by civilization. The Sharifian Empire had no surfaced roads, not a single mile of railway track, and a primitive commerce that went by mule and donkey over sandy trails. Foreign trade, which was conducted on a modest scale, was limited to a few ports. All the foreign commerce and investments existing or envisaged in the foreseeable future were hardly worth a war. Morocco became the focus of major controversy, however, not because of conflicting commercial and investment interests, but because the dispute over Morocco brought into play and helped to crystalize two of the major power rivalries of Europe, the Franco-German and the Anglo-German rivalries.

In this power struggle President Roosevelt was destined to play a major role. He was not drawn into the controversy by the necessity of protecting American interests in Morocco, which were insignificant, or primarily by the desire to de-

66

fend the interests of any other nation. His principal concern was to prevent the outbreak of a general European war. Once drawn into the dispute, however, he was to become so deeply involved that his participation would continue long after the danger of war had subsided.

It was the signing of the Entente Cordiale by Britain and France in April 1904 that set in motion the developments that brought Europe to the precipice of war in 1905. In concluding the Entente, Britain was motivated both by colonial aspirations and by the wider considerations of national security. Britain wanted a free hand in Egypt, and this was perhaps its primary motivation. But the rise of the German navy was ever present in the minds of most British leaders, and this, at times consciously, at times unconsciously, gave direction to their thoughts and actions. The Entente would mean more to Britain than a free hand in Egypt; it would bring it into close association with the Franco-Russian Alliance, the chief counterpoise to German power in Europe.

France likewise valued the Entente for both its colonial aspect and its larger meaning. France unquestionably intended to take over Morocco in one form or another. When Maurice Paléologue, Deputy Director of Political Affairs, asked Foreign Minister Théophile Delcassé on January 1, 1904, what he wished for the New Year, Delcassé included high on his list of wishes successful negotiations with Britain, Italy, and Spain on the Moroccan question. "You'll see Morocco drop into our lap," he confided to Paléologue, "as simply and easily as a ripe apple from a tree." Three months later when the Entente was concluded with Britain, the wider implications of the agreement were also on the minds of French leaders. Paléologue noted in his diary:[1]

> It is a preliminary to common action in European politics. Is it directed against Germany? In terms no. But by implication, yes, in that the principle of the balance of power in Europe is set up as a barrier to the ambitious aims of the German *bloc* and the programme of expansion of which it makes no secret.

---

[1] Maurice Paléologue, *Three Critical Years (1904–05–06)* (New York: Robert Speller and Sons, 1957), pp. 1, 39.

Paléologue's observation did not tell the whole story, for Delcassé hoped not merely to check German expansion but actually to roll back the borders of the Reich. The French Foreign Minister's "fondest dream," as Paléologue discerned some months later, was to recover the lost provinces of Alsace and Lorraine, which had been ceded to Germany at the end of the Franco-Prussian War of 1870–1871. He hoped to build a diplomatic combination so powerful that at some future time when Germany desperately needed the support or the neutrality of France, it would have to resign itself to restoring the lost provinces. "I think it is quite conceivable," Delcassé confided to Paléologue in November 1904, "that we shall recover Alsace-Lorraine some day, simply by diplomatic means alone and the sheer dynamic force of our alliances."[2]

German leaders sensed the wider implications of the Anglo-French Entente, which does much to explain the sharp reaction that ultimately came from Germany. For years the Eminence Grise of the German Foreign Office, Baron Friedrich von Holstein, had assured the leaders in Berlin that the conflicts of interest between Britain on the one hand and France and Russia on the other hand were too serious to be composed and that Germany could hold the balance in Europe; but now this hope had been all but shattered by the conclusion of the Entente Cordiale. At this juncture Holstein advanced another theory which eventually proved to be an even greater mistake than the previous miscalculation. He asserted that England could be intimidated into breaking its close association with France by being brought to the edge of war. Furthermore, he believed that the whole direction of French foreign policy could be changed simultaneously if only Germany forced a crisis over the Moroccan question. The Kaiser was skeptical, but Chancellor Bülow agreed with Holstein. Bülow therefore plunged forward dragging the reluctant Kaiser with him. Many years later he set down in his memoirs a clear statement of his aims:[3]

> I felt that I could prevent matters coming to a head, cause Delcassé's fall, break the continuity of aggressive French policy,

---

[2] Paléologue, *Three Critical Years*, pp. 138–139. *See also* pp. 41, 115.

[3] Bernhard von Bülow, *Memoirs of Prince von Bülow*, translated by F. A. Voigt, 4 vols. (Boston: Little, Brown & Co., 1931), *II*, 121.

knock the continental dagger out of the hands of Edward VII and the war group in England, and simultaneously ensure peace, preserve German honour, and improve German prestige.

Delcassé had left himself vulnerable to a move by Germany, for he had deliberately ignored that country while gaining the assent of other powers to the French program in Morocco. In February 1905 Delcassé realized for the first time that Germany was going to precipitate a crisis. A report arrived in Paris telling of remarks made to the French Chargé at Tangier, René de Chérisey, by the German Chargé, Baron von Kühlman:[4]

Since your agreement with England, and especially after your agreement with Spain, we have been expecting you to keep us posted about this new situation. But we couldn't help seeing that you are systematically ignoring us in your Moroccan policy. We have shaped our own policy accordingly.

Delcassé could justly deny that Germany had not been informed of France's agreement with London and one that subsequently followed with Madrid, but he could not skirt the fact that he had refused to take up the Moroccan question with Germany in a meaningful way. He had not even opened a discussion with Berlin regarding either the protection of German interests in Morocco or the granting of compensation elsewhere for the infringement of German interests which would likely result from France's program in Morocco. That German interests would likely be squeezed out of Morocco, or at least greatly circumscribed, was already apparent. By the end of 1904 a French banking group had gained control of the customs collections of the entire Sharifian empire, and the police and garrison of Tangier had been put under French administration.[5] Germany was thus in an excellent legal position to object to Delcassé's Moroccan policy; and with Russia pinned down in the war with Japan, it was apparently also in a good strategic stance.

Bülow decided to force a showdown by having the Kaiser visit the Moroccan port of Tangier. Paris first learned of this when in early

[4] Paléologue, *Three Critical Years*, p. 167.
[5] Eugene N. Anderson, *The First Moroccan Crisis, 1904–1906* (Chicago: University of Chicago Press, 1930), pp. 130–132.

March the Kaiser's aide-de-camp remarked to the French Naval Attaché at Berlin that on the Kaiser's approaching Mediterranean cruise His Majesty was going to call at "your Tangier." Delcassé was taken by surprise by this news, and he was dumfounded that Kaiser William was "daring to throw down the gauntlet at Tangier." [6]

Before the German ruler embarked upon his cruise, the Berlin government sought unsuccessfully to draw President Roosevelt into the Moroccan question. Ambassador Sternburg came to the White House on March 6 with a message from the German Emperor asking Roosevelt to tell the Sultan, as Germany was telling him, that the United States would support him in any opposition he might make to France in its attempt to obtain control of Morocco. It was the Kaiser's belief that France would not risk war with the Sultan if Germany and the United States indicated they supported his resistance to French demands. He also told Roosevelt that England would welcome a solution insuring the open door in Morocco and would therefore not support France.[7]

If the Kaiser's request meant what it apparently meant — that the United States should range its military and naval forces with Germany and Morocco against France — it was an astounding message indeed. Roosevelt, however, ignored the amazing import of the message and simply gave the Kaiser's entreaty a brief and polite rebuff. He told Speck that the interests of the United States were not sufficiently great that he could see his way clear to interfere in the matter. Were he to become involved in Morocco, a country entirely unknown to the American public, he would expose himself to the most severe attacks.[8]

---

[6] Paléologue, *Three Critical Years*, p. 185.

[7] Sternburg to Roosevelt, March 6 ,1905, A. L. P. Dennis, *Adventures in American Diplomacy, 1896–1906* (New York: E. P. Dutton & Co., 1928), pp. 513–514.

[8] Sternburg to the Foreign Office, telegram, March 9, 1905, Germany, Auswärtiges Amt, *Die Grosse Politik der Europäischen Kabinette, 1871–1914,* 40 vols. (Berlin: Deutsche verlagagesellschaft für politik und geschichte, 1922–1927), XX, 258–259 (translated in Dennis, *Adventures in American Diplomacy,* pp. 487–488); Roosevelt to Reid, April 28, 1906, Morison, *Roosevelt Letters, V,* 230.

Germany proceeded without American support. On March 31 the Kaiser made his dramatic landing at Tangier. He gave a speech at the German Legation avowing his determination to preserve the rights of Germany in a free Morocco, and he pointedly informed the French Chargé that he intended to maintain German interests. While the reverberations from the Tangier visit resounded throughout Europe, Germany instigated a call by the Sultan for an international congress on the Moroccan question.[9]

The Kaiser immediately sought Roosevelt's support for the conference project. On April 5 Sternburg sent to Roosevelt a long memorandum giving the German ruler's views. Germany, said the Emperor, must insist upon a conference; its dignity would not allow it to permit France to dispose of Germany's interests without asking for its consent.

> As soon as France discovers that Germany meekly submits to her bullying, we feel sure that she will become more aggressive in other quarters and we do not consider a demand for a revision of the Treaty of Frankfort to be far off.

The Emperor assured Roosevelt that Britain's support of France would not go beyond "diplomatic support." He believed that even diplomatic support was so contrary to Britain's interests in Morocco that it must have been promised some very valuable concession in return. That concession, thought the Kaiser, was a secret promise to support Britain's annexation of China's Yangtze valley.[10]

Roosevelt was on his hunting trip in the West when Sternburg's memorandum arrived, and Taft forwarded the message to him. In doing so Taft commented that he did not think the United States had interests in Morocco substantial enough to "range ourselves on the side of Germany." [11] Roosevelt agreed. He replied to Taft: "You are acting exactly right about Morocco." Taft was told to tell Speck that at present there was nothing for the United States to do on the

---

[9] Anderson, *First Moroccan Crisis*, pp. 181–206.

[10] Sternburg to Roosevelt, April 5, 1905, Dennis, *Adventures in American Diplomacy*, pp. 514–516.

[11] Taft to Roosevelt, April 5, 1905, Theodore Roosevelt Papers, Library of Congress, Washington, D. C.

matter and that Roosevelt would discuss it with him on his return to Washington. Roosevelt went on to indicate to Taft that he thought the suspicions about Britain taking the Yangtze valley ridiculous. "I wish to Heaven our excellent friend, the Kaiser," said Roosevelt, "was not so jumpy and did not have so many pipe dreams." [12]

The German government did not wait for Roosevelt's return to Washington before sending another plea for support on April 13. This time Germany asked specifically for the United States to use its influence in winning British agreement to attend a conference on Morocco. At Berlin it was believed that American influence would be decisive in dissuading Britain from supporting France. "England will not play an active part if only because of America," Baron von Holstein wrote to the German Ambassador at Paris.[13] Sternburg's letter of April 13 giving the Kaiser's second appeal to Roosevelt urged the President to give a confidential hint to England that the United States favored the convening of a conference. The attitude of England, he said, "would entirely depend on your attitude." [14]

The appeal from Germany brought a direct reply from Roosevelt revealing that he still wished to stay out of the controversy. "Our interests in Morocco," he wrote Sternburg on April 20, "are not sufficiently great to make me feel justified in entangling our Government in the matter." He did agree, however, to have Taft sound out the British government regarding its views.[15] This, of course, was not responsive to the German request, for he only said he would try to find out what Britain's policy was, not help shape that policy. In the subsequent days Taft made inquiry through Ambassador Durand, but the attempt to elicit information failed. It was on this occasion that Lans-

---

[12] Roosevelt to Taft, April 8, 1905, Elting E. Morison (ed.), *The Letters of Theodore Roosevelt,* 8 vols. (Cambridge, Mass.: Harvard University Press, 1951–1954), *IV,* 1158–1159.

[13] Holstein to Hugo von Radolin, April 11, 1905, Norman Rich and M. H. Fisher (eds.), *The Holstein Papers,* 4 vols. (Cambridge, England: Cambridge University Press, 1955–1963), *IV,* 329–332.

[14] Sternburg to Roosevelt, April 13, 1905, Dennis, *Adventures in American Diplomacy,* p. 516.

[15] Roosevelt to Sternburg, April 20, 1905, Morison, *Roosevelt Letters, IV,* 1165–1166.

downe pointedly informed Durand that he did not want Roosevelt mediating between Britain and Germany.[16]

Roosevelt returned from his hunting trip on May 11, and within two days Sternburg was at the White House with another communication from the German Emperor. It again urged Roosevelt to give a hint to Britain to drop its opposition to a conference and reiterated the theory that United States influence would be decisive in determining Britain's attitude. The Kaiser claimed that he had refused invitations from France to come to an agreement in which Germany would get advantageous compensation, for he wished to champion the cause of the whole world. He would be forced to think of Germany alone, he said, if he discovered that he would receive no support from the interested powers regarding the open door and the calling of a conference. Only then would he have to "choose between the possibility of a war with France and the examining of those conditions which France may have to propose, so as to avoid a war." He went on to speculate that Britain's support of Delcassé was part of a plan for a coalition of powers to partition China,[17] a supposition Roosevelt thought "mere lunacy."[18]

After his talk with Roosevelt on May 13, Sternburg reported to Berlin that the President expressed indignation over Britain's opposition to a conference and promised to explain his position to the British representative in Washington.[19] It is very doubtful, however, that Roosevelt said any such thing to Specky, for he had been very careful not to take sides with Germany. What confirms this further is the fact that two weeks later Roosevelt had said nothing to the British about the conference and the German government was still pleading with Roosevelt to give a hint to Britain. Sternburg sent

---

[16] Durand to Lansdowne, telegram, April 26, 1905, Lansdowne to Durand, telegram, April 27, 1905, G. P. Gooch and Harold Temperley, *British Documents on the Origins of the War, 1898–1914,* 11 vols. (London: His Majesty's Stationery Office, 1926–1938), *III,* 67–68.

[17] Sternburg to Roosevelt, May 13, 1905, Roosevelt Papers.

[18] Roosevelt to Reid, April 28, 1906, Morison, *Roosevelt Letters, V,* 231.

[19] Sternburg to the Foreign Office, telegram, May 13, 1905, *Die Grosse Politik, XX,* 622–623 (translation in Dennis, *Adventures in American Diplomacy,* pp. 489–490).

another memorandum to the White House on May 29, this one claiming that Britain and France had offered Germany a sphere of influence in Morocco if it would still the Moroccan question. The Emperor assured Roosevelt that his position remained unchanged; his policy was directed against the acquisition of territory and in favor of the open door and the maintenance of the status quo.[20]

Roosevelt betrayed no concern over the report that Germany was being offered a sphere in Morocco. He probably gave no credence to the German claim. If so, he was on sound ground, for Britain and France had made no such offer. During April France had made soundings for a general agreement — from which Bülow incorrectly inferred that France contemplated giving Germany a sphere in Morocco — but what France had in mind was giving compensation in some other colonial area where the two nations were already neighbors.[21]

On May 31 Sternburg sent still another message to Roosevelt repeating the now familiar theme. The Emperor did not regard Morocco as an isolated question but the starting point of a new grouping of powers. If Britain were successful in causing the refusal of France to join in a conference, Germany would have to choose between war with France or an understanding with France. England would drop its opposition to a conference if the United States agreed to participate.[22] To encourage Roosevelt further Sternburg, the next day, recalled in another note that the United States was one of the signatories to the international convention of 1880 relating to Morocco.[23]

Despite all the German pleas, Roosevelt declined to act on the request that he attempt to influence British policy. Not only did he refuse to take the side of Germany, he manifested marked leanings

---

[20] Sternburg to Roosevelt, May 29, 1905, Roosevelt Papers.

[21] Hugo von Radolin to Bülow, April 30 and May 1, 1905, Count Monts to the Foreign Office, telegram, May 2, 1905, *Die Grosse Politik, XX,* 355–357, 360–361, 362: Bülow, *Memoirs, II,* 128–133; Jean Jules Jusserand, *What Me Befell: The Reminiscences of J. J. Jusserand* (Boston and New York: Houghton Mifflin Co., 1933), p. 318.

[22] Sternburg to Roosevelt, May 31, 1905, Dennis, *Adventures in American Diplomacy,* p. 517.

[23] Sternburg to Roosevelt, June 1, 1905, Roosevelt Papers.

towards France. He was convinced that a civilized nation should take over Morocco, and France was the logical power to do it. He assured Ambassador Jusserand in early June that he was resolved to give France no trouble over Morocco.[24] His pro-French inclination was also evident in a letter he sent many months later to Ambassador Reid at London: "I desired to do anything I legitimately could for France; because I like France, and I thought her in this instance to be in the right. . . ."[25] Roosevelt also confided to Reid that he believed Speck did not approve of the action of his government, an observation that probably reveals more about Roosevelt's view than that of the German Ambassador.

If Britain entertained anxieties about Roosevelt's position on the conference question, they were soon dispelled. On June 5 Foreign Secretary Lansdowne promised the French Ambassador at London that he would sound the United States and urge it not to support the conference proposal. This he did on the same day.[26] Shortly before the British inquiry arrived in Washington, Roosevelt had already informed both Sternburg and Jusserand that the United States would not join in any conference unless France acquiesced, and this information was telegraphed to London on June 6.[27]

On the same day that Roosevelt sent his reassuring reply to the British inquiry, Foreign Minister Delcassé resigned at Paris. As the Moroccan crisis deepened in the spring of 1905, Delcassé had come under increasingly heavy criticism at home. France was simply in no position to risk war. In May Chief of Staff Pendézec had confided to Paléologue in a trembling voice: "A sudden attack by Germany! We couldn't resist it! It would be worse than 1870!"[28] Delcassé's cabinet colleagues agreed that he had gotten France into an untenable posi-

---

[24] Jusserand, *What Me Befell*, pp. 316–317; Jusserand to Prime Minister Maurice Rouvier, telegram, June 6, 1905, *Documents Diplomatique Francais,* 2nd. series, *VI,* 596–597.

[25] Roosevelt to Reid, April 28, 1906, Morison, *Roosevelt Letters, V,* 234.

[26] Lansdowne to Sir Frank Bertie, June 5, 1905; Lansdowne to Durand, June 5, 1905, *British Documents, III,* 89–90; Reid to the Secretary of State, telegram, June 5, 1905, Roosevelt Papers.

[27] Roosevelt to Reid, telegram, June 6, 1905, Morison, *Roosevelt Letters, IV,* 1207.

[28] Paléologue, *Three Critical Years,* p. 221.

tion. The matter came to a showdown when there arrived from London what Delcassé thought to be an offer of an alliance. On May 17 and again on May 25 Lansdowne had told Ambassador Paul Cambon that Britain and France should keep one another fully informed and discuss in advance any contingencies by which they might, in the course of events, find themselves confronted.[29] Cambon mistakenly read into Lansdowne's words an offer of an alliance.[30] When Delcassé attempted to go forward with the alliance project, Prime Minister Maurice Rouvier charged him with leading France into war. According to Rouvier, an emissary of Chancellor Bülow had told him that Germany knew of Delcassé's negotiations for an alliance and that if the alliance was concluded, Germany would immediately declare war. "You must not think that Germany is bluffing," Rouvier exclaimed to Delcassé at the crucial cabinet meeting on June 6. "She is both worried and humiliated by the isolation in which you are keeping her and the ring you have forged around her." Delcassé had no substantial support either in the Chambers or the cabinet, and at the end of the meeting he resigned.[31]

Prime Minister Rouvier thought that Delcassé's ouster would appease the German government sufficiently so that the Moroccan dispute could be settled in bilateral negotiations, but he was soon awakened from that dream. Germany continued to insist upon an international conference, and within a week of Delcassé's fall, France and Germany were again on the brink of war.

Roosevelt became aware of the seriousness of the crisis when he received a message from the German Emperor on June 11. It told of the British offer of an alliance to France and, incidentally, revealed that it was none other than Rouvier himself who had informed the German government of the alliance proposal. Neither the Kaiser nor Roosevelt, of course, knew that England had made no such offer, that

---

[29] Lansdowne to Bertie, May 17, 1905, Lansdowne to Cambon, May 25, 1905, *British Documents, III*, 76, 77–78.

[30] George Monger, *The End of Isolation: British Foreign Policy, 1900–1907* (London and New York: Thomas Nelson & Sons, 1963), pp. 196–199.

[31] Paléologue, *Three Critical Years*, pp. 243–249; Anderson, *First Moroccan Crisis*, pp. 230–231.

the whole matter resulted from Ambassador Cambon's misunder-standing of Lansdowne's words. The Kaiser declared to Roosevelt that Britain would back France by force of arms in order to smash the German navy and give the Entente powers and Russia a free hand in the Far East. He made it clear to Roosevelt that Germany would go to war unless France backed down. He asked the President to use his influence with the British to persuade them to agree to a conference. If Roosevelt did not feel inclined to take this step regarding the con-ference, said the German memorandum — and here followed the ominous words — "the Emperor believes that your influence could prevent England from joining a Franco-German war, started by the aggressive policy of France in Morocco."[32]

The German government was apparently in earnest. Just the day before Roosevelt received the Kaiser's message, the German Ambas-sador at Paris had told Rouvier that if France refused the conference and attempted to modify the status quo in Morocco in any way, Ger-many would support the Sultan with all its forces.[33]

The danger of war now brought Roosevelt to intervene in the con-troversy. He decided, however, to take up the question with the French rather than with the British, as suggested by Kaiser William. He agreed with the Kaiser that England was urging France on, but he believed he would have a greater chance of success in influencing the French rather than the British. He had already attempted to sound out London in April, only to receive a cool rebuff from Lansdowne. Moreover, he felt that the danger of war would be more keenly felt in Paris than in London, since the brunt of war with Germany would fall not upon Britain but upon France.

Roosevelt took his first important step when he called in the French Ambassador on June 14 and urged the acceptance of the conference proposal. He confided to Jusserand that Emperor William had asked him to persuade the British government to withdraw its opposition to the conference under the assumption that France would then have no choice but to fall in line. This he had declined to do because it

---

[32] Sternburg to Roosevelt, June 11, 1905, Morison, *Roosevelt Letters, V,* 235–236.
[33] Paléologue, *Three Critical Years,* p. 251.

would be an unfriendly act towards France; it would look as if he were trying to break up the Anglo-French Entente. He did, however, express disapproval of the London government for urging the French to resist when the British had no apprehension about a war in which they would have to play only an insignificant part on land and would secure easy gains with their navy. He thought there was but one chance in three that the Kaiser had the intention of going to war, but he regarded even such a limited possibility as serious. Roosevelt alluded to the reports that France was offering Germany a sphere of influence in Morocco, and he expressed the thought that a conference might be a better alternative: "I'm wondering if you wouldn't choose the lesser of two evils by agreeing to the conference." If the conference were held, he assured the Ambassador, France would have every reason to believe that the other participating nations would not sanction an unjust attack by Germany on French interests. As for himself, if the United States went to the conference, he would "take very strong grounds against any attitude of Germany which seemed to us unjust and unfair."[34]

Within a few days the danger of war would bring the French government to accept Roosevelt's advice. On June 16 Germany informed France that it would not discuss the Moroccan question until France accepted the Sultan's invitation to a conference. "This," commented Rouvier, "makes me believe what the Emperor said in his letter to Roosevelt — if we don't agree to the conference, war will be inevitable." The next day General Pendézec predicted: "The German armies, 1,500,000 strong will sweep over us in one great flood."[35] On the 19th Roosevelt cabled another plea to Paris: "What is needed is to give some satisfaction to the immeasurable vanity of William II and it would be wise to help him save face if thereby one can avert war."[36] In France the agonizing decision to accept a conference had

[34] Jusserand to Rouvier, telegram, June 14, 1905, *Documents Diplomatique Francais,* 2nd. series, *VII,* 68–70; Jusserand, *What Me Befell,* pp. 317–318; Paléologue, *Three Critical Years,* pp. 254–255; Roosevelt to Reid, April 28, 1906, Morison, *Roosevelt Letters, V,* 236.

[35] Paléologue, *Three Critical Years,* pp. 255–256.

[36] Jusserand to Rouvier, telegram, June 18, 1905 (received June 19, 1905),

apparently been made shortly before Roosevelt's latest message arrived. On the 18th Paul Cambon, who was in Paris at the time, remarked to Paléologue: "So we shall have to submit to a conference. I'm off to prepare Lansdowne for it; it will be extremely humiliating."[37]

Berlin discerned a change of attitude at Paris following Roosevelt's intervention, though it did not immediately receive France's formal assent to a conference. Sternburg informed Roosevelt on June 18 that he had received a telegram from his government which spoke of the marked change in French policy since Roosevelt's action with regard to the Morocco question. The Kaiser characterized the President's move as "the greatest blessing to the peace of the world."[38] The German government soon had further cause for delight. On June 23 France informed Roosevelt that it was now ready to accept the *idea* of a conference of powers on Morocco.[39] Roosevelt thereupon informed Sternburg that he had been informed that France had ceased its opposition to a conference. "Let me congratulate the Emperor most warmly on his diplomatic success," exclaimed Roosevelt. "It is a diplomatic triumph of the first magnitude."[40]

Roosevelt's congratulations were slightly premature. Although France had indicated to him that it would accept the *idea* of a conference, the Paris government withheld formal assent, insisting that Germany and France first settle various aspects of the Moroccan question in bilateral negotiations. France wanted, among other things, German recognition of its right to control the Moroccan police on the Moroccan-Algerian border and Germany's agreement not to attempt to undermine the rights France had recently secured in treaties with Britain, Spain, and Italy. The German government quickly discerned that the French government was holding back a formal acceptance of a conference. When Sternburg telegraphed

---

Documents Diplomatique Francais, 2nd. series, *VII,* 90; Jusserand, *What Me Befell,* pp. 318–319.

[37] Paléologue, *Three Critical Years,* p. 256.

[38] Sternburg to Roosevelt, June 18, 1905, Roosevelt Papers.

[39] Rouvier to Jusserand, telegram, June 23, 1905, *Documents Diplomatique Francais,* 2nd. series, *VII,* 117–119.

[40] Roosevelt to Sternburg, June 23, 1905, Morison, *Roosevelt Letters, V,* 238–239.

Berlin June 25 giving Roosevelt's message that France had agreed to a conference, the Kaiser noted on the telegram: "Not yet! A little bit 'previous' this letter!!"[41]

Roosevelt realized that there was more trouble ahead when Sternburg informed him on the evening of June 25 that France was holding back and that Germany could not agree to concessions prior to the conference.[42] Roosevelt thereupon undertook to break the deadlock. He urged the Kaiser not to raise questions about "minor details." Germany, he asserted, had won a "great triumph." It was on this occasion that Roosevelt warned that if Germany got involved in war with England it would lose all its colonies and the Kaiser's "high and honorable fame might be clouded." He also threw in all the flattery possible. "You know," he told Sternburg, "that I am not merely a sincere admirer and well-wisher of Germany, but also of His Majesty." The Kaiser, he said, "stands as the leader among the sovereigns of today who have their faces set toward the future."[43]

Roosevelt showed Jusserand his telegrams to the Kaiser before sending them, and he feared that the French might misunderstand his praise of the German ruler. "Let not people in France take it amiss," he assured Jusserand, "if I am found particularly flattering toward the Emperor." [44] The French government, however, could hardly have taken it amiss, for it knew that Roosevelt's sympathies were on the side of France. Prime Minister Rouvier told Jusserand to thank Roosevelt for his action and to inform him that it was his advice that brought France to accept the idea of a conference. The exceptional authority which was attached to the President's advice, said Rouvier, was due not only to his office but also to his character, understanding, and sense of justice, which qualified him in the highest degree to intervene in favor of peace.[45]

---

[41] Sternburg to the Foreign Office, telegram, June 25, 1905, *Die Grosse Politik, XX,* 473–475.

[42] Sternburg to Roosevelt, June 26, 1905, Roosevelt Papers. This message summarized what Sternburg told Roosevelt the previous day.

[43] Roosevelt to Sternburg, June 25, 1905, Morison, *Roosevelt Letters, IV,* 1256–1257.

[44] Jusserand, *What Me Befell,* p. 320.

[45] Rouvier to Jusserand, telegram, June 23, 1905, *Documents Diplomatique Francais,* 2nd. series, *VII,* 117–118.

Roosevelt agreed with the French government's position that it should pursue some form of guarantee of the rights it had gained in the treaties with Britain, Spain, and Italy. Jusserand informed Rouvier:[46]

> Mr. Roosevelt considers quite justified and wise the limit drawn by you. . . . We may accept a conference, and this is, certainly, a considerable concession, but we cannot go so far as to disown our previous engagements. . . .

Roosevelt even proposed to France and Germany a formula which, though somewhat ambiguous, was designed to give France what it wanted. It stated: "The two Governments consent to go to the conference with no program, and to discuss there all questions in regard to Morocco, save of course where either is in honor bound by a previous agreement with another power."[47]

Within a few days both sides began to soften; and as the two nations struggled for agreement on the conference question, Roosevelt received a remarkable commitment from Ambassador Sternburg. Bülow telegraphed Sternburg on June 27 that he expected France to agree to the conference shortly, and he went on to instruct Sternburg to tell Roosevelt that if difficulties should arise in the coming negotiations with France, he would be willing to advocate before the Emperor whatever decision Roosevelt recommended as practical and fair.[48] Bülow's promise was extraordinary enough, but in transmitting it Sternburg made it far more extraordinary. The Ambassador misread his instructions and did not tell Roosevelt merely that *Bülow* promised to advocate the views of Roosevelt. He informed Roosevelt that the *Emperor* promised to back up the decision Roosevelt considered practical and fair. Sternburg further misinterpreted his instructions to

---

[46] Jusserand to Rouvier, telegram, June 30, 1905, Jusserand, *What Me Befell,* pp. 320–321.

[47] Jusserand to Rouvier, telegrams, June 27 and 28, 1905, *Documents Diplomatique Francais,* 2nd. series, *VII,* 156–157, 178–181; Sternburg to the Foreign Office, telegram, June 27, 1905, *Die Grosse Politik, XX,* 480–481; Roosevelt to Reid, April 28, 1906, Morison, *Roosevelt Letters, V,* 240–241.

[48] Bülow to Sternburg, telegram, June 27, 1905, *Die Grosse Politik, XX,* 481–482.

mean that this commitment would apply during the conference, whereas Bülow had in mind only the Franco-German negotiations which would take place after France's formal acceptance of the conference but before the conference assembled.[49] Needless to say, Roosevelt was startled at receiving such a commitment. In writing to Senator Lodge he characterized it as "extraordinary" and said he would be "very wary" of availing himself of it.[50]

Despite Roosevelt's cautious attitude, he was to make decisive use of the German promise during the conference. He also put the commitment to immediate use in persuading France to give formal assent to the holding of a conference. He confided to Jusserand for transmission to Paris the exact words of Sternburg's statement.[51] In the preceding weeks he had made clear to the French government his pro-French sympathies, and when news arrived in Paris that he possessed something approaching a veto over German policy at the projected conference, it did much to incline France to accept a conference.

A week after Roosevelt's message arrived in Paris, the French and German governments reached an agreement for the holding of a conference. In the exchange of notes that took place on July 8 France did not gain all it wanted in the way of prior assurances, but it did obtain a recognition of her special interests in Morocco. Germany agreed not to propose at the conference anything which compromised the legitimate interests of France in Morocco or anything contrary to the rights of France resulting from her treaties, so long as those rights were in harmony with the principle of the independence of Morocco and the equality of economic opportunity there. Perhaps more important, Germany recognized the special interest of France in maintaining order in Morocco because of its contiguity to Algeria.[52] Negotiations continued following this exchange of notes, and in September Germany agreed that the supervision of the Moroc-

---

[49] Sternburg to Roosevelt, June 28, 1905, Morison, *Roosevelt Letters, V*, 241.

[50] Roosevelt to Lodge, July 11, 1905, Morison, *Roosevelt Letters, IV*, 1270–1273.

[51] Roosevelt to Jusserand, June 30, 1905, Roosevelt Papers.

[52] *British Documents, III*, 115–116; Anderson, *First Moroccan Crisis*, pp. 254–255.

can police on the Moroccan-Algerian border would be exclusively in the hands of France and Morocco.[53] In the subsequent weeks Algeciras, Spain, was chosen for the site of the conference. Thus the Moroccan question was committed to the conference table rather than to the field of battle.

From the beginning of his involvement in this dispute, Roosevelt had assumed that the United States would participate in a conference if it were held. When this became publicly known in the fall of 1905, it evoked vigorous discussion in the United States. After Congress assembled in December, Senator Augustus Bacon of Georgia introduced a resolution objecting to United States participation in the conference on the ground that it had been "the settled policy of this Government since its foundation to abstain from taking part in such political controversies between European nations." Lodge and other supporters of Roosevelt, however, managed to quash the Bacon resolution by burying it in the Foreign Relations Committee.[54]

The failure of the Bacon resolution assured American participation in the conference, but it did not assure Roosevelt a completely free hand to participate in a European quarrel. The concept of nonentanglement still dominated the thinking of the public, the press, and the Congress. Even before the opposition led by Senator Bacon materialized, Ambassador Jusserand had reminded his government of this fact. When in July Prime Minister Rouvier instructed him to secure from the United States government a pledge of its support at the coming conference,[55] Jusserand, instead of obeying his instructions, counselled the Prime Minister that there would be some problem and inconvenience in asking that the American representative side with France against Germany. It would be much better, he thought, simply to keep the good will of the President, who had

---

[53] British Documents, III, 143–144; Documents Diplomatique Francais, 2nd. series, VII, 586–588.

[54] Congressional Record, 59th. Congress, 1st. Session, XL, Part I, 792, 851, 946–948; Part II, 1069–1081, 1417–1423, 1469–1470, 1529–1530, 1755; Part III, 2139–2142.

[55] Rouvier to Jusserand, telegram, July 10, 1905, Documents Diplomatique Francais, 2nd. series, VII, 260.

already shown his sympathies for France.[56] Later, as the time for the conference approached, Jusserand renewed the advice to his government to be very circumspect in soliciting support from the United States. He told Rouvier that the French should not delude themselves into believing that American traditions and policies allowed entanglement in European difficulties unless circumstances were completely exceptional in view of certain American interests. Even in the latter case the United States would act independently. He was convinced that if news reached the American public that France expected American diplomatic support against Germany, so much opposition would be stirred up that Roosevelt's hands would be tied. He told his government bluntly that if by any unwise move France allowed the American public to think that the French government was counting on a certain action by the United States in France's favor, it would in advance render such an action unrealizable. In this matter, he said, France could not have too much reserve.[57] Jusserand never had the least doubt, however, that if France left matters to the natural course of events, Roosevelt would give strong support to France at the conference.

The correctness of Jusserand's expectations had meanwhile been underlined by the choice of Henry White as chief United States delegate to the conference. While considering whom to name to the American delegation, Roosevelt received from Lodge advice very much to his liking. "The local dispute in Morocco," said the Senator, "is a matter of indifference to us, but it is of very great importance to us to give France all the help that we can."[58] At Lodge's suggestion Roosevelt offered the post of chief delegate to Joseph Choate, and when Choate declined, the appointment went to White, who was serving at the time as Ambassador to Italy. White was left in no doubt concerning Roosevelt's own views, which happily coincided with his own. In a letter to White in August 1905, Roosevelt said: "I want to keep on good terms with Germany, and if possible to pre-

---

[56] Jusserand to Rouvier, telegram, July 13, 1905, *Documents Diplomatique Francais*, 2nd. series, *VII*, 260.

[57] Jusserand to Rouvier, January 10, 1906, *Documents Diplomatique Francais*, 2nd. series, *VIII*, 501–502.

[58] Lodge to Roosevelt, August 14, 1905, Roosevelt Papers.

vent a rupture between Germany and France. But my sympathies have at bottom been with France and I suppose will continue so."[59] To assist White, Roosevelt named as second delegate Samuel R. Gummeré, the United States Minister to Morocco. Gummeré was suspected of pro-German leanings, but his position and his expert knowledge of Morocco made his selection logical. Fortunately for Roosevelt and White, the suspicion that he was pro-German proved to be unfounded.

Elihu Root, who had been named Secretary of State following the death of Hay in July 1905, drafted the instructions to White and Gummeré. These formal instructions gave little hint of Roosevelt's pro-French attitude,[60] but Root sent a personal letter to White which was more revealing. The Secretary told White that he might find upon close inquiry that France had "legitimate interests by reason of her proximity to Morocco . . . which ought to be specially safe-guarded." The United States, he said, did not wish to become an advocate of those special interests, but it did not desire to oppose a provision for the protection of those interests. "In your consideration of this subject," Root said,[61]

> bear in mind that, while we are friendly to Germany, and wish to remain so, we regard as a favorable condition for the peace of the world, and, therefore, for the best interests of the United States, the continued Entente Cordiale between France and England, and we do not wish to contribute towards any estrangement between those two countries.

Root knew that White would welcome such instructions. He confided to Jusserand the substance of the instructions and added: "You know White, and you can imagine whether he will conform with pleasure to such instructions."[62]

---

[59] Roosevelt to White, August 23, 1905, Morison, *Roosevelt Letters, IV,* 1313.

[60] Root to White and Gummeré, November 28, 1905, Instructions to Special Agents, *IV,* 410–414, Department of State Records, National Archives, Washington, D. C.

[61] Root to White, November 28, 1905, Elihu Root Papers, Library of Congress, Washington, D. C.

[62] Jusserand, *What Me Befell,* p. 322; Jusserand to Rouvier, telegram, received January 12, 1906, *Documents Diplomatique Francais,* 2nd. series, *VIII,* 519–520.

If Roosevelt or Root had any serious apprehensions that the Anglo-French Entente might be weakened, nothing had thus far occurred to substantiate such fears. On the contrary, the Moroccan dispute had strengthened rather than weakened the Anglo-French connection. Paléologue noted in his diary that "with the vision of the German menace clearly before their eyes, France and England have realized as never before that a close association is a necessity."[63] White expressed a similar view in a letter to Roosevelt:[64]

> The Germans have had their way in that matter [the holding of a conference], but in so doing they have greatly strengthened the Franco-English understanding, which is the very last thing the Emperor can have wanted.

Germany became aware of just how much the Entente Cordiale had been strengthened when the new Liberal government in England read it a warning late in 1905. Although the new Foreign Secretary, Sir Edward Grey, refused to give a definite assurance of support to France,[65] he said enough to the German Ambassador to cause concern in Berlin. He told Ambassador Paul von Metternich bluntly that if war broke out over Morocco, public feeling in England would be so strong in favor of France that it would be impossible for England to remain neutral.[66]

As the time for the conference approached, Roosevelt hoped he would be able to help Europe prevent the outbreak of general war, but he realized the limitations of his influence. In a letter to Ambassador Reid at London he explained that where there was a chance to prevent trouble by preventing misunderstanding, his intervention might prove helpful. On the other hand, if there was a genuine conflict of interest in which each side was resolved to carry its point at the cost of war, there was no use in his interfering.[67] To Spring Rice he wrote

---

[63] Paléologue, *Three Critical Years,* p. 267.
[64] White to Roosevelt, August 10, 1905, Roosevelt Papers.
[65] Grey to Bertie, January 31, 1906, *British Documents, III,* 180–181.
[66] Grey to Lascelles, January 9, 1906, *British Documents, III,* 209–211; Monger, *The End of Isolation,* pp. 268–269.
[67] Roosevelt to Reid, August 3, 1905, Morison, *Roosevelt Letters, IV,* 1297–1298.

that if he saw that he could contribute to the peace in Europe, he would certainly do so, but he did not wish to assume the position of an international "Meddlesome Mattie" or to make himself ridiculous by interfering where his interference would be rebuffed or ineffective. At the time Roosevelt penned this letter to Spring Rice, he was basking in the success of the Portsmouth Peace Conference, but the messages of congratulations which had deluged the White House had not completely turned his head. He assured Springy that he did "not intend to go into peacemaking as a regular business." It was enough, he observed, to keep the United States on an even keel.[68]

Roosevelt's modest appraisal of his influence in international affairs was doubtless sincere and generally accurate. Still, Reid and Spring Rice knew Roosevelt well enough to discern that it would not take much to convince him that he should intervene in the coming conference. What they did not know was that Roosevelt had more influence to wield than merely that accorded to the United States by virtue of its independent position in world politics. He had a written promise from the German Ambassador giving him the right to dictate German policy. It would take a measure of restraint beyond that possessed by Roosevelt to keep him from playing that card in the exciting game about to begin at Algeciras.

---

[68] Roosevelt to Spring Rice, November 1, 1905, Morison, *Roosevelt Letters, V,* 61–64.

The Algeciras Conference

5

In January 1906 delegates of thirteen countries assembled at the half-Spanish, half-Moorish town of Algeciras, Spain, which lay in the shadow of Britain's fortress at Gibraltar. The envoys were as varied as the conflicting national interests that brought them together. From England came a lone representative, Sir Arthur Nicolson, who had previously served at Tangier and was now Ambassador to Spain. Bent with arthritis and the weight of protecting an empire, Sir Arthur was still a perceptive and skillful diplomat. From France came M. Paul Révoil, a small, ever-smiling gentleman who had once been governor-general of Algeria. He was a highly trained lawyer given to subtle and wordy argumentation, a characteristic which led Nicolson to observe: "Révoil is most childish and irritating with his formulas and 'artifices de redaction' as if the Germans were asses enough to be deceived by a cloud of words."[1] Russia sent Arturo Cassini, the former Russian Ambassador to Washington. Henry White knew him and neither liked nor trusted him, an attitude Roosevelt fully shared. From Italy came the most command-

---

[1] Sir Harold Nicolson, *Portrait of a Diplomatist; Sir Arthur Nicolson, Bart., First Lord Carnock: A Study in the Old Diplomacy* (Boston and New York: Houghton Mifflin Co., 1930), p. 137. A delightful description of the participants is given in Lewis Einstein, *A Diplomat Looks Back,* Lawrence E. Gelfand, (ed.) (New Haven: Yale University Press, 1968), pp. 3–24. Einstein served as secretary to the United States delegation.

ing personality of the conference, Marquis Visconti Venosta. A hero of the *risorgimento* and former Foreign Minister of Cavour, he was the embodiment of Italy's modern history. White greatly enjoyed his talks with Venosta, while the Marquis envied White's freedom of action.[2] The venerable Italian was in an awkward position at the conference, with Italy bound to Germany by the Triple Alliance and obligated to France by a secret treaty concluded in 1902 giving France a free hand in Morocco in return for an Italian free hand in Tripoli. The Spanish government sent its Foreign Minister, the Duke of Almadovar, who was elected president of the conference. White made a special effort to be cordial to the Duke in order to help smooth over the ill-feeling resulting from the Spanish-American War.

To this assemblage of notables, Germany named Joseph von Radowitz and Count von Tattenbach. Chancellor Bülow had written in November 1905 that Germany's main object at the conference must be to avoid diplomatic isolation,[3] and if this indeed was the German policy, two more unfortunate appointments could hardly have been made. Radowitz, the senior German delegate, was aging and feeble, and too weak in character to hold in check the fiery Tattenbach. Tattenbach, who was a special favorite of Baron von Holstein, was rude and ill-tempered.[4] He was certainly not the man to bring to reality the grand dreams of the leaders in Berlin, which included visions of gaining American support and of detaching Britain from the support of France.

The primary issue at the conference was the organization of the police in the principal ports of Morocco. The Sharifian empire had shown itself utterly incapable of protecting foreigners in the port cities, and all the powers agreed that some kind of foreign supervised police system must be established. Even before the convening of the conference, the major powers had been jockeying for position on

---

[2] Allan Nevins, *Henry White: Thirty Years of American Diplomacy* (New York: Harper & Bros., 1930), p. 269.

[3] Memorandum by Bülow, November 23, 1905, Germany, Auswärtiges Amt, *Die Grosse Politik der Europäischen Kabinette, 1871–1914,* 40 vols. (Berlin: Deutsche verlagagesellschaft für politik und geschichte, 1922–1927), XXI, 14–15.

[4] Nicolson, *Portrait of a Diplomatist,* pp. 127, 134, 140.

this issue. In September 1905, it will be recalled, Germany recognized France's right to help Morocco supervise the police on the Moroccan-Algerian border. There remained the question of what power or powers would command the police in the port cities. France wished to control the police, though it was willing to allot a subordinate share in the administration to Spain. In the same month that France and Germany concluded the agreement on the border police, France and Spain signed a secret agreement whereby the officers of the police would be French in two ports, Spanish in two ports, and French and Spanish in the principal port of Tangier. Concurrently Spain pledged its unqualified support to France and Britain at the conference.[5]

It was just this kind of police administration that Germany was determined to prevent. A week before the conference opened, Sternburg relayed from Berlin a long memorandum to Roosevelt asserting that the only question which might create dangerous complications during the conference was that touching the organization of the police. Said the German message:[6]

> To grant to France a mandate to establish the police within the whole country of Morocco would render the principle of the open door absolutely illusory, because with the police France would receive the whole administration.

When the conference began its formal deliberations on January 16, it took up first a series of non-controversial questions to allow time for informal talks among the principal delegates on the crucial police question. It was obvious from the outset that a deadlock existed. White, who served as liaison between the French and German delegates, conferred with the German envoys and found them adamant in opposing French and Spanish control of the police.[7] The German

---

[5] France, Ministère des Affaires Etrangères, *Documents Diplomatique Francais 1871–1914),* 2nd. series (Paris: Imprimerie Nationale, 1930–1955), 2nd. series, VII, 511–517.

[6] Sternburg to Roosevelt, January 8, 1906, Theodore Roosevelt Papers, Library of Congress, Washington, D. C.

[7] Nicolson to Grey, telegram, January 21, 1906, G. P. Gooch and Harold Temperley, *British Documents on the Origins of the War, 1898–1914,* 11 vols. (London: His Majesty's Stationery Office, 1926–1938), *III,* 231.

government was unsure, though, of what to propose as a substitute. Berlin was apparently desperate to seize upon any alternative to French and Spanish control. On January 23 Sternburg sent Roosevelt a message suggesting three possible schemes: (1) each major power take over the policing in one port; (2) the policing be given to one or several minor powers; or (3) the Sultan organize the police with the aid of foreign volunteer officers selected by the Sultan or by the minor powers.[8]

Roosevelt and Root were suspicious from the beginning that while opposing a French mandate on the police, Germany was scheming to secure a sphere in Morocco. When Root relayed the German proposals to White, he explained that he had informed Sternburg that the United States considered "wholly inadmissible" the suggestion that each major power police one port.[9] White agreed, and he advised Root that the two other German suggestions were also unsatisfactory. White had become convinced, however, that it would be impossible to secure Germany's assent to a French police administration. He reported to Root that he had, therefore, been seeking the assent of the delegates to a compromise plan whereby the police administration would be assigned to Italy. He believed that such a solution was agreeable to Germany, Britain, and Italy, but he had been unable thus far to gain French assent.[10]

The opposition of France prevented White from going further with his proposal, and on January 28 Germany presented to Roosevelt still another plan. The Berlin government now suggested that the Sultan be entrusted with the organization of the police with an international commission to manage the necessary funds. The proposal was not clear concerning how the foreign officers in the police administration would be selected. In fact, it was not clear from Sternburg's text of the German proposal whether foreign officers were to be used at

[8] Sternburg to Roosevelt, January 23, 1906, Roosevelt Papers.

[9] Root to White, telegram, January 23, 1906, Instructions to Special Agents, IV, 421–424, Department of State Records, National Archives, Washington, D. C.

[10] White to Root, telegram, received January 26, 1906, Despatches from Special Agents, L, 68–70, Department of State Records, National Archives, Washington, D. C.; Nicolson to Grey, January 26, 1906, Nicolson to Grey, telegrams, January 27 and 28, 1906, British Documents, III, 238–240.

all.[11] Root immediately telegraphed White for his views on the vague German plan and his opinion concerning whether France would accept it. Washington's lack of enthusiasm for the scheme was apparent in Root's telegram. "We would not under any circumstances make such a proposal," said Root, "if it involved responsibility for seeing it carried out, and it is difficult to see how we could make the proposal without assuming some such responsibility."[12]

White was even more unenthusiastic than Root and Roosevelt. He had taken the lead in arranging direct talks between the French and German delegates, and they had not yet taken up the police question. He advised Root, therefore, that it would be premature to bring forward any proposal. Furthermore, he was convinced that France would reject the scheme now proposed by Germany because it would involve some German participation in the police financing system.[13]

When Révoil and Radowitz met to discuss the police issue a few days later, they made no progress toward a solution. Révoil refused even to discuss the matter except on the basis of French and Spanish control. France, he told Radowitz, would give every guarantee as to the open door for economic enterprise, but it must have, with Spain, the supervision of the police.[14] After the meeting Radowitz recounted Révoil's words to White and observed that it was clear that France would go no further than to divide the police administration with Spain. White concurred, advising Radowitz that it would be useless to treat on any other basis. Radowitz thereupon asked White if he thought France would agree to a third power being associated in the policing duty. White said he did not think so, though he thought that France might accept a third power as a nominal inspector.[15]

Meanwhile Tattenbach, the second German delegate, had attempted to detach Britain from supporting France. He called on

---

[11] Sternburg to Roosevelt, January 28, 1906, Roosevelt Papers.

[12] Root to White, telegram, January 29, 1906, Instructions to Special Agents, IV, 424–425.

[13] White to Root, telegram, received January 30, 1906, Despatches from Special Agents, L, 89.

[14] White to Root, telegram, February 5, 1906, Despatches from Special Agents, L, 104.

[15] Nicolson to Grey, telegram, February 6, 1906, British Documents, III, 244.

Nicolson on February 3 and told him that the commercial interests of Germany and England were endangered by French predominance in Morocco and that Germany and England should join forces to secure the open door. He even went so far as to tell Nicolson that if he did not urge Révoil to give in on the police question, Britain would be responsible for the failure of the conference. Nicolson was incensed both by what Tattenbach said and the manner in which he said it. He told Tattenbach flatly that he had not the least fear that British commercial interests were in danger and that he intended to stand firmly by Révoil. That Tattenbach's overture had made the German position worse rather than better was evident in comments Nicolson sent to his wife soon after the meeting: "Tattenbach nearly made me lose my temper. . . . He is really a horrid fellow, blustering, rude, and mendacious. The worst type of German I have ever met."[16] To White he exclaimed: "The damned Germans have had the audacity to offer us inducements to get us away from France!"[17]

German efforts to gain support from Russia and Italy were equally unsuccessful. Russia was badly in need of a foreign loan, which she hoped to get from France. Count Witte explained this to his German friends and added that European opinion was beginning to credit Germany with a desire to humiliate France. At Rome Germany lodged a complaint that Venosta was leaning toward France, but the action served only to stir the anger of the venerable Italian delegate. The German Ambassador at Rome advised his government that the Marquis was not so much a Francophile as a realist, and Chancellor Bülow soon realized that he had only made matters worse by sending the complaint to the Italian government.[18]

By the end of the first week of February, it was obvious that Germany had little support at the conference. The powers were simply not alarmed at the prospect of France moving into Morocco to bring order to that troubled land. Back in June 1905, Roosevelt had told

---

[16] Nicolson, *Portrait of a Diplomatist,* pp. 133–134.

[17] Nevins, *Henry White,* p. 272.

[18] Serge Witte, *The Memoirs of Count Witte* (Garden City, N. Y.: Doubleday, Page & Co., 1921), pp. 298–301; Nicolson, *Portrait of a Diplomatist,* p. 136; White to Roosevelt, April 8, 1906, Roosevelt Papers.

Sternburg that people in the United States would gladly see Morocco rendered civilized by some foreign power,[19] and it was apparent at Algeciras that the other countries shared this view. France was willing to give Spain a subordinate role in the policing and to give assurances regarding the open door; this was enough to satisfy all the delegates but those of Germany and Austria. Although it was not clearly perceived by all the powers, by early February the only real question at the conference was to what extent and by what formula would Germany be permitted some face-saving.

White took the lead in seeking some means of salvaging German prestige. On February 5 he had first suggested to the German senior delegate that a third power might be given a nominal inspectorship over the police administration, and he now repeated the suggestion on February 8. On that day he discussed the police question with Radowitz at length and he emphasized that Germany would have to yield. He reminded Radowitz that he preferred that Italy organize the police but that his attempts to secure a settlement along that line had failed. "We must now face facts," White said bluntly. If Germany would accept France and Spain as the policing powers, he would try to obtain agreement for the appointment of a third power to a nominal position in the police administration to "save German prestige."[20]

During the negotiations, which had now continued for three weeks, White became convinced that the German government was not receiving accurate reports from its delegation. It was equally apparent to White that Berlin was receiving inaccurate information from the German Embassy in Washington. In his talk with Radowitz on February 8, the German delegate told him that Sternburg had reported that Roosevelt favored Germany's proposal for having the Sultan organize the police with the aid of volunteer officers from the minor powers. Radowitz even believed that White had been instructed to support him. White correctly discerned that Sternburg had badly

---

[19] Sternburg to the Foreign Office, telegram, June 8, 1905, *Die Grosse Politik, XX,* 421.

[20] White to Root, telegram, received February 9, 1906, Despatches from Special Agents, *L,* 107–108.

misinformed his government; thus he refused to associate himself with the German proposal. In reporting the incident to Washington on February 9, White said he doubted whether the Kaiser was "frankly informed of actual conditions here."[21]

White's statement that the Kaiser was poorly informed led Roosevelt and Root to consider some action. Until he received White's telegram of February 9, Root had been very wary of the United States taking an important initiative. Root had instructed White that the United States desired to avoid putting itself forward "in any manner which might appear to be not justified by the very general character of our interest in the subject."[22] Roosevelt had expressed a similar view, though doubtless with a good deal less conviction. He wrote to Ambassador Meyer on February 1: "I do not know that I can do anything if the circumstances become strained at Algeciras, and of course I want to keep out of it if I possibly can."[23] But now with White's report that Berlin needed to be told of the unpleasant realities at the conference, the attitude of hesitancy disappeared at Washington. "If you think any independent statement of the situation ought to reach German Emperor," Root telegraphed White on February 10, "let me have it and I will see that it reaches him."[24]

White immediately replied that he had detected a softening of the German position and that any communication to the Kaiser should be delayed.[25] White was convinced, however, that when the proper time came, Washington should take action. White then proceeded to outline the realities for Root and Roosevelt. France, he said, would accept no other principle but a Moroccan police commanded

---

[21] White to Root, telegram, received February 9, 1906, Despatches from Special Agents, L, 107–108.

[22] Root to White, telegram, February 9, 1906, Instructions to Special Agents, IV, 426–427.

[23] Roosevelt to Reid, February 1, 1906, Elting E. Morison (ed.), The Letters of Theodore Roosevelt, 8 vols. (Cambridge, Mass.: Harvard University Press, 1951–1954), V, 145.

[24] Root to White, telegram, February 10, 1906, Instructions to Special Agents, IV, 427.

[25] White to Root, telegram, received February 11, 1906, Despatches from Special Agents, L, 109.

by French and Spanish officers in the ports. France, believed White, dared not yield for fear of impairing and possibly destroying the Anglo-French Entente. A considerable section of French opinion was already lukewarm or antagonistic to the understanding with Britain, and if France had to retreat on the vital police issue, the Entente would appear to be of little value to France. White was convinced that the conference would fail unless Germany could be brought to accept the French position.[26]

While Roosevelt and Root awaited news that the time was right for intervention, White attempted to break the deadlock at Algeciras. On February 13 he conferred with Radowitz concerning a German proposal to have the Sultan organize the police with officers chosen freely by him from any foreign powers. Under this plan a superior officer of one of the minor powers would make periodic inspections and report to the diplomatic body at Tangier. White warned Radowitz that France would reject the proposal in that form, but he expressed the thought that certain features of the plan might serve as a basis for negotiations. Later the same day he met with Révoil after the French delegate had received the German proposal. At that meeting White made his ideas more explicit. He pointed out that if the words "French and Spanish officers" were substituted for "foreign officers" in the German proposal, there seemed very little to which France might not assent. He went on to warn the French delegate that if any agreement was to be attained, France must assent to a third power in some nominal capacity in order to save German prestige.[27]

On February 17 France accepted White's advice. On that day Révoil informed the German delegation that if "French and Spanish officers" could be inserted in place of "foreign officers," the French government was willing to examine the question of the nationality of a supervisory officer.[28] At the same time the French delegation

---

[26] White to Root, telegram, received February 11, 1906, Despatches from Special Agents, L, 110–111.

[27] White to Root, telegram, February 14, 1906, Despatches from Special Agents, L, 137–139.

[28] White to Root, telegram, received February 17, 1906, Despatches from Special Agents, L, 140.

confided to White that it would agree to have the French and Spanish officers make reports to Italy for communication to the powers.[29] Thus the French opened the door to some kind of nominal supervision of the police by a third power. The next move was up to Berlin.

White now telegraphed Washington that the time had arrived for Roosevelt's intervention; his advice was immediately followed. On February 19 Roosevelt sent a message to the Kaiser in the form of a letter from Root to Sternburg. In essence it proposed the pro-French plan which White had been hammering out at Algeciras. Roosevelt used phraseology, however, which was designed to maintain the fiction that he was responding to Germany's previous request to present the German plan. Root's letter explained that Roosevelt thought the time had arrived for him to present to the conference the German proposal that the organizing of the police be entrusted to the Sultan. Before doing so, the President wanted the German government's assent to some "details." Root then listed the details, which actually converted the German proposal into White's pro-French plan. The police were to be organized by the Sultan, who would employ French and Spanish officers for "duties of instructions, discipline, pay and assisting in management and control." The senior French and Spanish officers would report to Italy annually and that government would have the right of inspection and verification and the right to demand further reports on behalf of the powers. Regarding the international bank for Morocco, which the conference proposed to establish, the stock would be allotted to all the powers equally "except for some small preference claimed by France." Regarding the open door, it was proposed that France and Spain give full assurances concerning equal commercial and investment opportunity.[30] This latter suggestion was the only important feature that supported the German position and it was not a controversial issue. France had from the beginning offered to give such assurances.

The Kaiser's reply, which arrived in three days, gave assent to all Roosevelt's proposals except the crucial item regarding French and

---

[29] White to Root, telegram, received February 17, 1906, Despatches from Special Agents, L, 141–143.

[30] Root to Sternburg, February 19, 1906, Morison, *Roosevelt Letters,* V, 243.

Spanish control of the police. Placing the police forces entirely in the hands of France and Spain, said the Kaiser, would mean a monopoly which would heavily curtail the political and economic positions of other nations. He went on to suggest that the Sultan be permitted a free choice of police officers from among all the countries. In order to allay French fears that the Sultan might favor German officers, said the Emperor, it could be stipulated that the officers be taken from at least four different nationalities on an equal basis and the French might be given police control in Tangier.[31]

Roosevelt's intervention, at least for the moment, had failed to win German assent to White's plan, but the German position was already beginning to crumble. On the very day Roosevelt received the German message, Chancellor Bülow informed Holstein that neither the German public, parliament, princes, nor even the army would have anything to do with a war over Morocco. "Everything depends on our seizing the right moment for an acceptable compromise," he commented realistically.[32] Even the usually imperturbable Holstein was losing his confidence. On March 4 he expressed the wish for an agreement with France if "only the French should not want to gobble up the whole of Morocco at once."[33] Neither Roosevelt nor the delegates at Algeciras realized that German resolve was weakening. On the contrary, it appeared that the Franco-German impasse was hardening. Nicolson telegraphed London on March 3 that the failure of the conference seemed inevitable.[34] Two days later White telegraphed Washington that a rupture was imminent.[35]

White's telegram now stirred Roosevelt to invoke the promise which Sternburg had given many months before that Germany would be bound by his advice during the conference. He had al-

---

[31] Sternburg to Roosevelt, February 22, 1906, Morison, *Roosevelt Letters*, V, 244.

[32] Bülow to Holstein, February 22, 1906, Norman Rich and M. H. Fisher (eds.), *The Holstein Papers*, 4 vols. (Cambridge, England: Cambridge University Press, 1955–1963), IV, 396–397.

[33] Holstein to Bülow, March 4, 1906, *Holstein Papers*, IV, 399.

[34] Nicolson to Grey, telegram, March 3, 1906, *British Documents*, III, 282–283.

[35] White to Root, telegram, received March 5, 1906, Despatches from Special Agents, L, 185–186.

ready proffered advice on February 19 without mentioning the promise, only to have the vital proposal on the police rejected. He wrote to Reid on March 1, "As my experience has always been that a promise needlessly entered into is rarely kept, I never expected the Kaiser to keep this one, and he has not." [36] Now when it appeared that the conference might fail, Roosevelt decided to remind Berlin of its commitment in unequivocal language. He dispatched a telegram to the Kaiser on March 7 which quoted verbatim Sternburg's letter of June 28, 1905, committing the Kaiser to back up in every case the decision Roosevelt considered the most fair and the most practical. The proposals of February 19, he said, were reasonable and France should not be expected to go further. Attempting to put the matter in the best possible light, he assured the Kaiser that such an arrangement "would be in very fact the evidence of the triumph of German diplomacy in this matter." [37]

Roosevelt's message caused consternation in Berlin. Bülow realized for the first time the sweeping nature of Sternburg's letter to Roosevelt of June 28, 1905. With much irritation and bewilderment he telegraphed the Ambassador on March 12 that in giving the promise to Roosevelt he (Sternburg) had exceeded his instructions in two ways. He had been authorized to say only that Bülow promised to advocate before the Kaiser the proposals Roosevelt considered fair, but he had confirmed acceptance in the name of the Kaiser himself. Furthermore, Sternburg had committed Germany to take Roosevelt's advice during the conference, while Bülow had had in mind only the pre-conference negotiations between Germany and France. The Chancellor knew that Sternburg's inexplicable blunder had placed Germany in an almost hopeless position. If it were impossible to disavow the letter, Bülow telegraphed Sternburg, "his Majesty will probably hardly be able to avoid accepting the present proposal of the negotiations of President Roosevelt upon his repeated urging to do so." [38]

---

[36] Roosevelt to Reid, March 1, 1906, Morison, *Roosevelt Letters, V,* 169–170.
[37] Root to Sternburg, March 7, 1906, Morison, *Roosevelt Letters, V,* 245–246.
[38] Bülow to Sternburg, telegram, March 12, 1906, *Die Grosse Politik, XXI,* 276–278.

The invoking of Sternburg's promise proved to be a decisive influence at Algeciras, not only because it brought German capitulation, but because it helped to create conditions that made the German defeat greater than it otherwise would have been. Roosevelt confided to Jusserand that he had invoked the promise, and news of this was immediately sent to Paris and from there to the French delegation at Algeciras. The result was a significant hardening of the French position. White telegraphed Root on March 7 that the French were greatly stiffened by confidential information from the French Ambassador at Washington that the President had addressed a strong communication to the German Emperor that was based on "a sort of promise . . . to accept, in case of deadlock, the former's decision as final." [39]

Roosevelt was alarmed by the news that the German promise of June 28, 1905, had been revealed to any of the delegates at Algeciras. He immediately called in Jusserand and told him it would be very harmful if the German Emperor learned that his secret promise had been revealed. He might use its revelation, Roosevelt warned, as a pretext to deny a promise which was supposed to remain secret. A wounding of his pride would in any case put him in as bad a disposition as possible for concessions. Roosevelt went on to urge the greatest prudence on the part of the French. Roosevelt's views were immediately sent to Paris, along with the news that Root would telegraph White to reduce to the most modest proportion the importance of the matter. [40]

As Jusserand dispatched his telegraphic report to Paris, Root's telegram was on its way to White at Algeciras. In it Root declared that the President's communication to the Emperor was not based on any promise, and White was instructed to correct the misunderstanding discreetly. [41] But of course there had been no misunderstanding

---

[39] White to Root, telegram, received March 7, 1906, Despatches from Special Agents, L, 188–189.

[40] Jusserand to Rouvier, telegram, received March 9, 1906, Documents Diplomatique Francais, 2nd series, IX, 535.

[41] Root to White, telegram, March 8, 1906, Instructions to Special Agents, IV, 441.

and the French position remained rigid. The telegram did, however, check the further revelation of the German promise. Roosevelt and Root soon learned from White, much to their relief, that it had been revealed only to White and Nicolson and would not be revealed to any other delegations.[42]

Developments at Algeciras enabled the German government to parry Roosevelt's move temporarily. The day after Roosevelt invoked the promise, Austria introduced a new compromise plan, and discussion was now focused upon it. Austria, after gaining prior assent from Germany, proposed that French officers administer the police in four ports, the Spanish in three ports, and a Swiss or Dutch officer be appointed inspector general over all ports and have the direct administration over police at Casablanca. This Austrian proposal was a concession to France of major proportions and it unleashed hopes for a successful conclusion of the conference. In reporting the Austrian scheme to Washington, White said that general opinion at the conference was favorable, with even the Russian and British delegates thinking it might, with modifications of detail, be accepted by France. France, ran the consensus of the delegates, could not afford to break up the conference by rejecting it.[43]

White accurately assessed the sentiment at Algeciras. Nicolson reported to London that the members of the conference, with the exception of the French and Spanish, were unanimously in favor of the Austrian proposal. Nicolson reported, however, that the French were adamant in their refusal to assent to a Swiss or Dutch police administration at Casablanca.[44] This disturbed the British government so much that Foreign Secretary Grey told French Ambassador Cambon that the Austrian proposal had brought an agreement so near that "it would not do to let the Conference break up now without a settlement." [45] At Algeciras Nicolson gave a similar warn-

[42] White to Root, telegram, received March 10, 1906, Despatches from Special Agents, *L*, 193–194.

[43] White to Root, telegram, received March 8, 1906, Despatches from Special Agents, *L*, 191–192.

[44] Nicolson to Grey, telegram, March 9, 1906, *British Documents, III,* 288–289.

[45] Grey to Bertie, telegram, March 9, 1906, *British Documents, III,* 289.

ing to the French delegation.[46] Révoil reported to Paris that he was being pressed from all sides to give in.[47]

The French government nevertheless continued to maintain the unyielding stance it had adopted since learning of Roosevelt's invocation of the promise of June 28, 1905. White reported on March 12 that Révoil felt sure that Germany would yield further "through the President's intervention or otherwise." [48] In the face of French intransigence, British leaders could only wring their hands and continue to give at least outward support. Grey wrote privately to Ambassador Bertie in Paris:[49]

> You can see that even the 'Times' correspondent at Algeciras thinks France ought not to break off on such a wretched point as Casa Blanca, which I believe is a useless hole. However, if she does, we shall back her up. . . .

The French government hoped that Roosevelt would side with it on the Casablanca issue, despite all the pressure being exerted by other governments in favor of the Austrian proposal. That hope was to be fulfilled. While Britain urged France to yield, Roosevelt gave full support to the Paris government. When the Kaiser wrote to Roosevelt on March 13 urging the acceptance of the Austrian plan,[50] he got nowhere. Roosevelt told Sternburg that the proposal was absurd and would lead to partition and spheres of influence.[51] A few days later Roosevelt unburdened himself to Speck in even more forceful terms. He accused Germany of both trying to humiliate France and scheming to gain a sphere of influence and a port on the Moroccan coast. He told Sternburg to inform the Kaiser that he

---

[46] Nicolson to Grey, March 10, 1906, *British Documents, III,* 294–295.

[47] Révoil to Rouvier, telegram, March 12, 1906, *Documents Diplomatique Francais,* 2nd series, *IX,* 565–567.

[48] White to Root, telegram, March 12, 1906, *Despatches from Special Agents, L,* 196.

[49] Grey to Bertie, March 15, 1906, *British Documents, III,* 304–305.

[50] Sternburg to Roosevelt, March 13, 1906, Morison, *Roosevelt Letters, V,* 246–247.

[51] Sternburg to the Foreign Office, telegram, March 14, 1906, *Die Grosse Politik, XXI,* 285–286.

was reluctant to fill the role of intermediator because the world would regard him as a busybody, a reputation which, said Roosevelt, he already had in the United States.[52] The same day that this conversation occurred, Root sent a long letter to Sternburg reiterating the President's opposition to the Austrian proposal.[53]

Roosevelt was genuinely afraid that Germany was seeking a sphere and possible outright acquisition of Moroccan territory. "We became convinced," he later wrote to Ambassador Reid at London, "that Austria was a mere cat's paw for Germany, and that Germany was aiming in effect at the partition of Morocco. . . ." [54] The French government feared the same, and of this the German government was aware. Bülow wrote to Holstein on March 14, after talks with Baron Alphonse de Courcel, former French Ambassador at Berlin:[55]

Behind the French effort to exaggerate the importance of the Casablanca issue there apparently lies the fear, which Courcel has repeatedly expressed, that we intend to smuggle our Trojan Horse into Morocco through this port, with all the ensuing consequences that the French imagination can conceive.

It is doubtful, however, that at this late stage of the Moroccan dispute Germany was attempting to get a sphere or to acquire Moroccan territory. In 1905 Holstein had speculated about the possibilities in correspondence with Prince Hugo von Radolin, the German Ambassador at Paris,[56] but the Kaiser's opposition to such schemes was well known to German leaders.[57] Holstein confided to Radolin in August 1905 that if the German government pursued any plans involving territorial acquisitions in Morocco, it would be disavowed by

---

[52] Sternburg to the Foreign Office, telegram, March 17, 1906, *Die Grosse Politik, XXI,* 300–302.

[53] Root to Sternburg, March 17, 1906, Morison, *Roosevelt Letters, V,* 247–248.

[54] Roosevelt to Reid, April 18, 1906, Morison, *Roosevelt Letters, V,* 242.

[55] Bülow to Holstein, March 14, 1906, *Holstein Papers, IV,* 400–401.

[56] Holstein to Radolin, August 4, 1905, Radolin to Holstein, August 5, 1905, *Holstein Papers, IV,* 359–363.

[57] Bernhard von Bülow, *Memoirs of Prince von Bülow,* translated by F. A. Voigt, 4 vols. (Boston: Little, Brown & Co., 1931), *II,* 139–140.

the Kaiser, "who just now has a positive horror of Africa because of the revolts everywhere." [58]

If Bülow or Holstein had any designs on Moroccan territory — which is doubtful — they soon gave them up in the face of France's intransigence and Roosevelt's invocation of Sternburg's promise of June 28, 1905. On March 17 Nicolson reported to Foreign Secretary Grey that the way was being prepared at Algeciras for a further German concession.[59] That same day White telegraphed Washington that Germany was preparing to yield on the question of police at Casablanca.[60] These assessments were accurate, for on the day they were sent from Algeciras, Bülow wrote Holstein, "I concede that you were right when you said yesterday that we can in the end hardly make a *conditio sine qua non* out of Casablanca." [61]

As the Berlin government prepared to give way, Roosevelt tightened the screw another turn and forced it to yield. He told Sternburg on March 18 that if the conference failed, he would feel obligated to publish the entire correspondence.[62] Such a move, of course, would reveal Sternburg's promise of June 28, 1905, and Germany's betrayal of that commitment. Publication of the promise alone would have been extremely embarrassing to the German government, to say nothing of the revelation that it had been given and violated. The result was an immediate telegram from Berlin agreeing to a Franco-Spanish police administration at Casablanca. Bülow

---

[58] Holstein to Radolin, August 22, 1905, *Holstein Papers, IV,* 364.

[59] Nicolson to Grey, March 17, 1906, *British Documents, III,* 310–311.

[60] White to Root, telegram, received March 17, 1906, Despatches from Special Agents, *L,* 198–199.

[61] Bülow to Holstein, March 17, 1906, *Holstein Papers, IV,* 401. Holstein rather consistently opposed retreat, but by March 16 Germany had already retreated so far that it appeared to him that she could not stand firm on the Casablanca question. Bülow on March 12 declared to his associates that Germany must retreat, but he still contemplated holding out on the Casablanca issue until his letter to Holstein on March 17. Norman R. Rich, *Friedrich von Holstein, 2 vols.* (Cambridge, England: Cambridge University Press, 1965), *II,* 740–741.

[62] Roosevelt to Reid, April 28, 1906, Morison, *Roosevelt Letters, V,* 249; Sternburg to the Foreign Office, telegram, March 18, 1906, E. T. S. Dugdale, *German Diplomatic Documents, 1871–1914,* 4 vols. (London: Methuen & Co., Ltd., 1928–1931), *III,* 246–247.

ended his telegram with the statement that the "maintenance of the mutual trust between Berlin and Washington and immediate removal of all cause of misunderstanding are more important than the whole matter of Morocco." [63] Characteristically Roosevelt attempted to ease the German humiliation with flattery. "Inform His Majesty the Emperor," he told Sternburg, "of my heartiest congratulations on this epoch-making political success at Algeciras. His Majesty's policy in the Morocco question has been masterly from beginning to end." In reporting Roosevelt's remarks to Berlin, Sternburg commented: "Even though the foregoing does not appear to agree with the facts, I am firmly convinced that the words spoken by the President came entirely from the heart." [64] Sternburg was indeed a true friend not to see through such patent flattery.

Two more weeks passed before the Algeciras conference completed its work. Part of that time was consumed in unscrambling a complication unwittingly injected by Roosevelt's intervention. In prodding Germany to give in on the Casablanca issue, Roosevelt had made a strong stand against all possible spheres, French and Spanish as well as German. In his communications to the German government he put forward a proposal, which was actually suggested by Sternburg, that French and Spanish police officers be mixed in all the ports.[65] All proposals made at the conference up to that time, however, left the distribution of police officers up to France and Spain. When on March 19 Germany capitulated to Roosevelt's demands, it did so on the understanding that the French and Spanish officers would be divided roughly on an equal basis in each of the ports.[66] When the French, Spanish, and British delegates at Algeciras learned of Roose-

---

[63] Bülow to Sternburg, telegram, March 19, 1906, Dugdale, *German Diplomatic Documents, III*, 247–248; Sternburg to Roosevelt, March 19, 1906, Morison, *Roosevelt Letters, V*, 248–249.

[64] Sternburg to the Foreign Office, March 21, 1906, Dugdale, *German Diplomatic Documents, III*, 248.

[65] Root to White, telegram, March 14, 1906, Instructions to Special Agents, IV, 434; Root to Sternburg, March 17, 1906, Morison, *Roosevelt Letters, V*, 247–248.

[66] Sternburg to Roosevelt, March 19, 1906, Morison, *Roosevelt Letters, V*, 248–249.

velt's proposal for a mixed police administration at each port, they immediately expressed strong objection. Sir Edward Grey characterized it as an unworkable plan which introduced unfortunate complications. He remarked to the Austrian Ambassador that "there were too many peacemakers at work." [67]

The Paris government instructed Jusserand to see the President and get him to instruct White not to support the proposal for a mixed administration in each port. Foreign Minister Léon Bourgeois said bluntly to Jusserand that he (Jusserand) did not understand the goal France was aiming at. He went on to put forth the farfetched thesis that Germany had been on the point of giving in to France on the police issue before Roosevelt's intervention on February 19 and that therefore France should not be expected to make any concessions.[68] Jusserand knew better than to repeat such a specious claim, but he immediately set about untangling the diplomatic snarl. On March 23 he conferred with Roosevelt and Root at the White House in the afternoon and again in the evening. At the first meeting he found Roosevelt only mildly irritated, but before Jusserand returned in the evening British Ambassador Durand made inquiries on the issue.[69] This further embarrassed Roosevelt and turned his irritation into anger. What most disturbed him was that the French had left him in ignorance regarding what kind of police system they wanted and thus allowed him to stumble into an awkward situation. In the evening meeting Roosevelt exclaimed to Jusserand, "Your people have been less frank with me than I have been with you." Roosevelt indicated that he would have been quite willing to propose whatever police system France preferred if he had been informed ahead of time.[70] His remarks made it clear that his concern had been the pre-

---

[67] Grey to Sir Edward Goschen, March 21, 1906, *British Documents, III,* 315–316.

[68] Foreign Minister Léon Bourgeois to Jusserand, telegram, March 22, 1906, *Documents Diplomatique Francais,* 2nd. series, *IX,* 674–676.

[69] Grey to Durand, telegrams, March 22 and 23, 1906, F. O. 115/1391, and Durand to Grey, telegram, March 23, 1906, F. O. 115/1395, Public Record Office, London, England.

[70] Jusserand to Bourgeois, telegrams, March 23 and 24, 1906, *Documents Diplomatique Francais,* 2nd Series, *IX,* 691–692, 699–701.

vention of a German sphere, not a French or Spanish sphere. In Jusserand's presence he now drafted a telegram to White which supported the French position. It stated that although the mandate to France and Spain should be understood to be a joint one, the distribution of officers in the ports "should be settled as a matter of detail" between France and Spain.[71]

Jusserand blamed the Quai d'Orsay rather than Roosevelt for the mix-up. He sent a blistering report to his superiors which stopped just short of calling them incompetent. He pointed out how he had often complained to the department about the "skinny" instructions he received. (Calling them "skinny," he once told the department, was exaggerating in an optimistic sense!)[72] He said that he had often been left in ignorance of the views of his government during the Moroccan affair and that he hoped in the future to be informed in a very precise manner concerning the intentions of France. He pointed out that if the President had been forewarned, it was certain he would have taken France's desires into account. The miscalculation of the last few days, he lamented, had been a serious step backwards, for he had never seen the President in such a mood or such a disposition.[73] Jusserand was doubtless correct in his estimate of Roosevelt's irritation, for the President's later thoughts on the Moroccan dispute reflected his disgust at the last minute mix-up over distribution of the police. After the conference was over, he told White that Jusserand was a "trump" but that towards the end of the conference neither Germany nor France was straightforward.[74]

Fortunately the German delegates at Algeciras did not insist upon a mixed police administration in every port. They found France and her friends united against it, and even Austria did not favor it.[75]

---

[71] Root to White, telegram, March 23, 1906, Instructions to Special Agents, *IV*, 438–439.

[72] Jusserand to Delcassé, January 25, 1905, *Documents Diplomatique Francais*, 2nd. series, *VI*, 61–64.

[73] Jusserand to Bourgeois, March 25, 1906, *Documents Diplomatique Francais*, 2nd series, *IX*, 723–725.

[74] Roosevelt to White, April 30, 1906, Morison, *Roosevelt Letters, V*, 251–252.

[75] Grey to Sir Edward Goschen, March 23, 1906, *British Documents, III*, 318–319.

Therefore in the plenary session of March 26, when the German delegation formally relinquished the demand that a third power administer the police at Casablanca, it did not demand the mixed police system in every port.[76]

Germany's capitulation on the police issue was thus complete, and in the last days of March the details of the police system and other issues were quickly settled. France and Spain agreed upon the distribution of police in the ports, and the conference approved the arrangement. Four ports would have French police officers, two ports would have Spanish police officers, and the two remaining ports would have a mixed administration of French and Spanish officers. A Swiss rather than a Dutch inspector general was to be appointed. On the bank question it was agreed that each signatory would be allotted two shares and that a French banking syndicate which held extensive rights in Morocco would be given two shares for surrendering its rights to the new Moroccan bank. The open door for commerce and capitalistic investment was guaranteed for thirty years.[77]

The completed treaty was signed on April 6, at which time the United States extricated itself from any entanglements which might arise in connection with the enforcement of the treaty. On instructions from Root, White read a declaration to the plenary session stating that the United States, having no political interest in Morocco, signed the treaty "without assuming obligation or responsibility for the enforcement thereof." [78] After the conference was over, the United States took another step away from involvement in the settlement. It elected not to take the shares in the Moroccan bank which were available under the terms of the treaty.[79]

Despite the official disclaimer by the United States of a political interest in Morocco, Roosevelt's own role in the dispute had been

---

[76] Nicolson to Grey, telegram, March 26, 1906, *British Documents, III*, 321.

[77] Text of treaty is in United States, Department of State, *Papers Relating to the Foreign Relations of the United States, 1906*, 2 vols. (Washington, D. C.: Government Printing Office, 1909), *II*, 1495–1513.

[78] Root to White, telegram, April 5, 1906, Instructions to Special Agents, *IV*, 442–443.

[79] White to Root, telegram, May 5, 1906, Despatches from Special Agents, *L*, 398–399.

vigorous and decisive. In 1905, when a serious danger of war existed, he played a key role in obtaining agreement for the holding of an international conference. Once the conference met he did much to bring about a French victory, which in turn removed the danger that the Entente Cordiale might be weakened. It is difficult to imagine how he could have given more aid to the French during the Algeciras negotiations. Roosevelt forced Germany to give way on the Casablanca question at a time when even France's Entente partner Britain was ready to compromise.

Roosevelt's contribution to peace was limited largely to the events of 1905, for it was only in the pre-conference period that the danger of war was great. When the conference assembled in January 1906, the Germans were in no mood to push matters to the point of war, and this attitude persisted and even became stronger as the conference progressed. Roosevelt must have sensed this, at least in the later stages of the conference. Otherwise it seems doubtful that he would have risked forcing upon the Germans what was virtually total diplomatic defeat.[80]

Both Roosevelt and Root were aware that the American intervention had done much to determine the extent of the German humiliation. After the conference ended, Root told Ambassador Durand that it was the United States that had blocked Germany's attempt to gain a port opposite Gibraltar when Britain did not seem to mind.[81] Four years later when Roosevelt visited Britain, he told Sir Edward Grey that his own action had had great if not decisive influence in making Germany give way about the port of Casablanca.[82] A letter Roosevelt sent to Ambassador Reid in June 1906 is equally revealing of Roosevelt's own view of the role he had played: "In this Algeciras matter you will notice that while I was most suave and pleas-

---

[80] Norman Rich observes regarding the extent of the defeat: "Rarely has a state still capable of inflicting military defeat on her enemies been subjected to so complete a diplomatic defeat as that suffered by Germany at the Conference of Algeciras." Rich, *Holstein, II,* 742.

[81] Sir Percy M. Sykes, *The Right Honourable Sir Mortimer Durand* (London: Cassell & Co., Ltd., 1926), p. 301.

[82] Sir Edward Grey, *Twenty-five Years, 1892–1916,* 2 vols. (New York: Frederick A. Stokes Co., 1925), *I,* 118.

ant with the Emperor yet when it became necessary at the end I stood him on his head with great decision." [83] And indeed he had.

In retrospect it appears questionable whether Roosevelt should have driven the Germans to such a point of humiliation as resulted from their capitulation on the Casablanca issue. His fears that Germany was at that time scheming for a sphere or a port had little foundation. If Germany could have been spared that final humiliation at the conference, the delegates could have parted with more good will than they did. If the Austrian compromise plan had been accepted with minor changes, as everyone except the French and Roosevelt wished, the conference might have restored some tranquility to European international relations and made the Germans somewhat less sensitive to what they regarded as encirclement. It is true that an improved diplomatic atmosphere would have been of little importance unless it led to a resolution or easing of the fundamental conflicts of interest, such as Alsace-Lorraine and naval rivalry, but at least it would have been a step in the right direction.

It must be conceded on the other side, however, that Roosevelt's position on the Casablanca issue was the safest so far as future quarrels over Morocco were concerned. Though it is unlikely that Germany was scheming for a sphere or a port in 1906, there was no guarantee that it would not do so in the future. A Dutch police administration at Casablanca, the port where German interests predominated, would have left the door ajar for a future German move. Germany, with a ruler like William II, was unpredictable. His policies, as Roosevelt surmised, were subject to irrational zig-zags. The settlement Roosevelt secured in the Moroccan crisis at least had the virtue of simplicity. There were no serious obstacles to the eventual takeover of most of Morocco by France. And this is the way Roosevelt wanted it. Two and a half years after the Algeciras conference he felt the same way. He told Jusserand at that time: "As for the Moorish business, I wish to Heaven, not in your interest but in the interest of all civilized mankind, that France could take all Morocco under its exclusive charge." [84]

---

[83] Roosevelt to Reid, June 27, 1906, Morison, *Roosevelt Letters, V,* 318–320.
[84] Roosevelt to Jusserand, August 3, 1908, Morison, *Roosevelt Letters, VI,* 1147–1148.

In 1911–1912 France established a protectorate over all Morocco, except for a strip which became a Spanish protectorate. Roosevelt, as could be anticipated, wholeheartedly approved of the French takeover. As French troops marched on Fez in April 1911 he wrote to Charles D. Willard: "It would be enormously to the benefit of the people of Morocco if the French took hold of them and did for them what they have done in Algiers." [85] By the time France moved to set up the protectorate, its interests were so firmly established that Germany did not even attempt to prevent it. All the Berlin government felt able to do was to rattle its naval armaments loudly in order to gain colonial compensation elsewhere. This it secured in Central Africa in the form of a slice of the French Congo, a small compensation for all the losses Germany had suffered in the controversy over Morocco.

---

[85] Roosevelt to Charles D. Willard, April 28, 1911, Morison, *Roosevelt Letters*, *VII*, 256.

Britain versus Germany, 1906–1909

6

The summer of 1906 was a time of calm after the fury of the Moroccan dispute. Before the year ended another storm would come, the Japanese-American crisis over immigration; meanwhile Roosevelt had a few months for unhurried contemplation of the European rivalry and America's relation to it. In June he read with interest a letter from Ambassador Reid stating that "our relations with England are of far greater importance to us than those with Germany." Reid detected nothing to be gained from unusually good relations with Germany which could compensate for the least jar in relations with Britain.[1] With this general thesis Roosevelt agreed. He replied to Reid that he liked the Kaiser and the Germans and wished to keep on good terms with them but that it was even more important to keep on good terms with the English. He was "immensely amused," he said, at the European theory that he was taken in by the Kaiser.[2]

Actually Roosevelt was more than amused at the idea that he was under the influence of the Kaiser. He was annoyed by it. He was, however, partly responsible for the miscon-

---

[1] Reid to Roosevelt, June 19, 1906, Royal Cortissoz, *The Life of Whitelaw Reid,* 2 vols. (New York: Charles Scribner's Sons, 1921), *II,* 330–332.

[2] Roosevelt to Reid, June 27, 1906, Elting E. Morison (ed.), *The Letters of Theodore Roosevelt,* 8 vols. (Cambridge, Mass.: Harvard University Press, 1951–1954), *V,* 318–320.

ception, for a warm letter, which he sent to the Kaiser thanking him for aid in bringing peace between Russia and Japan, could only create an impression of unusual intimacy between Washington and Berlin. The British, of course, would not have been so ready to believe that Roosevelt was working in close cooperation with Germany if they had known the full story of his part in the Moroccan dispute, but they knew very little of this. Roosevelt had confided in Jusserand and Sternburg throughout the negotiations, but he had refused to confide in Durand because, as he told Ambassador Reid, he considered Durand "entirely incompetent for any work of delicacy and importance." [3]

In the summer and fall of 1906 Roosevelt undertook to correct the British misconception of his attitude. First he instructed Reid to show to King Edward and to Foreign Secretary Grey a forty-two page letter he had earlier sent Reid giving a full account of his role in the Moroccan dispute.[4] Then he invited his old friend Arthur Lee to visit Washington so that Lee could relay his views to British leaders. He hoped that through Lee's visit he could also remove what he considered the main obstacle to effective communication with London, for he intended to inform British leaders through him, as well as through Ambassador Reid, that Durand should be replaced. Lee came to Washington in October 1906 and in talks at the White House learned the whole story of Roosevelt's role in the Russo-Japanese peace negotiations and the Moroccan dispute, as well as the unhappy history of the Roosevelt-Durand relationship. After Lee's departure from Washington, Roosevelt sent word through Ambassador Reid that London ought to recall Durand and replace him with Lee as Ambassador to Washington if Spring Rice could not be appointed.[5]

Even before Lee returned to England, Grey himself took an initiative for closer contact with Roosevelt. Spring Rice's friend, Bob Ferguson, brought Roosevelt a message from the Foreign Secretary asking the President's advice on the projected Second Hague Peace

---

[3] Roosevelt to Reid, April 28, 1906, Morison, *Roosevelt Letters, V,* 251.

[4] Roosevelt to Reid, April 28 and June 27, 1906, Morison, *Roosevelt Letters, V,* 230–251, 318–320.

[5] Roosevelt to Reid, November 6, 1906, Morison, *Roosevelt Letters, V,* 488.

Conference. Roosevelt responded with a long friendly letter to Sir Edward giving his thoughts on arbitration and disarmament.[6] Soon after receiving Roosevelt's letter, Grey conferred with Lee and received the detailed statement of Roosevelt's views. Grey in turn sent Roosevelt on December 4 a long letter in which he freely opened his mind to the President. He confided at the outset that he had concluded even before conferring with Lee that Durand was not suited for diplomatic work and that he had to be replaced. He then gave Roosevelt a frank analysis of British policy. Britain wished to strengthen the Entente with France. To complete the formation she wished also to make an arrangement with Russia to ensure that if Britain and Russia could not be close friends, at least they need not quarrel. In pursuing this objective, wrote Grey, London would be careful not to provoke Germany, if only Germany accepted the situation and did not try to make mischief. Grey concluded with observations that echoed Roosevelt's own ideas on the kinship of the English-speaking peoples. Britain and the United States, he said, were bound by common language and religion but even more by the generations of freedom on both sides which had produced a type of man and mind that looked at things from a kindred point of view.[7]

Lee's visit to Washington and the initiation of the Grey-Roosevelt correspondence did much to clear up misconceptions among British leaders. Lee felt that Grey, "like nearly everyone else in England," had entirely misunderstood Roosevelt's relations with the Kaiser, but Lee believed he had now blown away the mist of misunderstanding.[8] Lee's visit also spurred on the replacement of Durand, a step which would help to prevent future misunderstandings. In a few months James Bryce would arrive in Washington to begin an ambassadorship marked by friendly relations with the American President.

While opening correspondence with Grey in 1906, Roosevelt continued the friendly exchange of messages with King Edward which

---

[6] Roosevelt to Grey, October 22, 1906, Morison, *Roosevelt Letters*, V, 462–464.

[7] Grey to Roosevelt, December 4, 1906, Theodore Roosevelt Papers, Library of Congress, Washington, D. C.

[8] Lee to Roosevelt, November 28 and December 24, 1906, Roosevelt Papers.

had begun the previous year. He gained a direct link with the monarch when the King's cousin, Colonel Count Gleichen, came to Washington in early 1906 as Military Attaché. Spring Rice, who was a close friend of Count Gleichen, thought he would get on famously with Roosevelt, for he was "absolutely fearless" [9] and had been shot in the stomach and the neck.[10] Like Durand, however, the Count found the President a bit overwhelming. After lunching at Oyster Bay several times and listening to Roosevelt dash from one subject to another in a "fast Yankee accent," he reported to the King with some bewilderment that "one certainly gets the impression of a powerful personality." [11]

During the summer of 1906, while Roosevelt, with characteristic verve, was developing new contacts with British leaders, he revealed his pro-British and anti-German attitude in his thoughts on naval limitation, a subject that arose in connection with plans for the Second Hague Peace Conference. In early 1905 Sternburg had reported Roosevelt's delight that the German navy was being strengthened,[12] but if Roosevelt had indeed expressed such notions in 1905, he believed emphatically otherwise by the summer of 1906. In letters to American diplomats in Europe and to British friends, he stated that he did not wish to see Britain's naval superiority weakened. "I should like to see the British navy kept at its present size," he told Ambassador Reid, "but only on condition that the Continental and Japanese navies are not built up. I do not wish to see it relatively weaker to them than is now the case." [13] To Henry White he ex-

[9] Spring Rice to Mrs. Roosevelt, January 4, 1906, Stephen Gwynn, *The Letters and Friendships of Sir Cecil Spring Rice: A Record,* 2 vols. (Boston and New York: Houghton Mifflin Co., 1929), *II,* 24.

[10] Spring Rice to Grey, n.d., Gwynn, *Letters and Friendships of Sir Cecil Spring Rice, II,* 25.

[11] Count Gleichen to Edward VII, February 8 and August 31, 1906, Sir Sidney Lee, *Edward VII, A Biography,* 2 vols. (New York: The Macmillan Co., 1925–1927), *II,* 436–438.

[12] Sternburg to Bülow, February 10, 1905, Germany, Auswärtiges Amt, *Die Grosse Politik der Europäischen Kabinette, 1871–1914,* 40 vols. (Berlin: Deutsche verlagagesellschaft für politik und geschichte, 1922–1927), *XIX,* 570–575.

[13] Roosevelt to Reid, August 7, 1906, Morison, *Roosevelt Letters, V,* 348–349.

pressed the view that it would be "a great misfortune for the free peoples to disarm and leave the various military despotisms and military barbarisms armed." [14] That he included Germany in the reference to "military despotisms" there is little doubt, for in a letter to Oscar S. Straus he characterized Germany as an aggressive military power that despised the whole Hague idea.[15] To George Otto Trevelyan he wrote that though he was interested in the Hague Conference, he did not feel that England and the United States should impair the efficiency of their navies if other potentially hostile powers were permitted to increase their military strength.[16] Roosevelt made clear his thoughts a few months later in a letter to John St. Loe Strachey, editor of the *Spectator*. He observed that although there had been foolish and irresponsible talk on both sides of the Anglo-German rivalry, it was nevertheless true that the German attitude toward war, fundamentally the Bismarck attitude, was one that in the progress of civilization England and the United States had outgrown.[17]

As the time for the convening of the Hague Conference approached in 1907, the continuing Anglo-German rivalry made prospects for accomplishment bleak. Roosevelt hoped that something might be achieved on limiting naval armaments, but Germany categorically refused to discuss the subject and Britain equivocated. Andrew Carnegie, who undertook to promote his peace campaign through the conference, pleaded with the Germans to relent, but in May 1907 Chancellor Bülow announced that Germany would not discuss arms limitation. In England Carnegie found some cabinet members, including Prime Minister Campbell-Bannerman, favoring limitation, but others, including Grey, "very offish." [18] Meanwhile Carnegie's activities had stirred up additional antagonism between

---

[14] Roosevelt to White, August 14, 1906, Morison, *Roosevelt Letters, V,* 359.

[15] Roosevelt to Straus, February 27, 1906, Morison, *Roosevelt Letters, V,* 168.

[16] Roosevelt to Trevelyan, August 18, 1906, Morison, *Roosevelt Letters, V,* 366.

[17] Roosevelt to Strachey, February 22, 1907, Morison, *Roosevelt Letters, V,* 596.

[18] Carnegie to Roosevelt, July 31, 1907, quoted in Howard K. Beale, *Theodore Roosevelt and the Rise of America to World Power* (Baltimore: Johns Hopkins Press, 1956), p. 345.

London and Berlin. He repeated to Roosevelt, and then to Ambassador Sternburg, a statement by a British cabinet member that the Kaiser was hostile to the Hague Conference and that the German ruler had asserted that the build-up of the German navy was directed against the United States.[19] On hearing of this the German Emperor dashed off a lurid telegram to Roosevelt accusing the British of telling "foul and filthy lies" in order to sow distrust between himself and Roosevelt.[20] If Sternburg's report of Roosevelt's response was accurate, the President sought to soothe the excited monarch not only by assuring him of his confidence in the Emperor's genuine friendliness to the United States but also by making allusion to "amateur" members of the Liberal cabinet in London.[21]

This incident, together with Britain's refusal to limit the size of warships and Germany's refusal even to discuss limitation, cooled Roosevelt's interest in the Hague Conference. In the fall of 1906 he had sent word to King Edward through Count Gleichen that he intended to support England to the utmost at the conference,[22] but once the negotiations began in the summer of 1907, he tended to ignore them. "I have not followed things at The Hague," he confessed to Root in July 1907.[23] The American delegation therefore received no direction from Roosevelt, and it sided with Germany on a number of questions relating to neutral rights in maritime warfare, much to the irritation of some members of the British delegation.[24] Roosevelt nevertheless remained convinced that Britain's policy of maintaining great naval superiority was "quite proper." [25]

---

[19] Roosevelt to Reid, January 10, 1907, Morison, *Roosevelt Letters, V,* 543–544.

[20] William II to Roosevelt, telegram, n.d., Morison, *Roosevelt Letters, V,* 544.

[21] Sternburg to the Foreign Office, telegram, January 6, 1907, *Die Grosse Politik, XXIII,* 94–95; Roosevelt to William II, January 8, 1907, Morison, *Roosevelt Letters, V,* 542–543.

[22] Count Gleichen to Edward VII, August 31, 1906, Lee, *Edward VII, II,* 437.

[23] Roosevelt to Root, July 2, 1907, Morison, *Roosevelt Letters, V,* 699–700.

[24] Eyre Crowe to William G. Tyrrell, October 11, 1907, G. P. Gooch and Harold Temperley, *British Documents on the Origins of the War, 1898–1914,* 11 vols. (London: His Majesty's Stationery Office, 1926–1938), *VIII,* 287–288.

[25] Roosevelt to Root, July 2, 1907, Morison, *Roosevelt Letters, V,* 699–700. A detailed account of Roosevelt and the Hague Conference is given in Beale, *Theodore Roosevelt and the Rise of America to World Power,* pp. 337–354.

Meanwhile the new British Ambassador, James Bryce, had arrived in Washington. When he presented his credentials on February 25, 1907, the President tossed aside the formal remarks drafted by the Department of State and made a long impromptu speech full of expressions of friendship for Britain.[26] Bryce had met Roosevelt and Root on previous visits to the United States and liked them both. Durand had always characterized Roosevelt as impulsive, but Bryce was more charitable. He reported to London that the President combined two qualities not usually united, impulsiveness and astuteness — impulsiveness in speech, astuteness in action.[27] Most of the new Ambassador's dealings were with Root. Together the two diplomats tackled the perennially troublesome North Atlantic fisheries question, and through long but genuinely friendly negotiations they reached accord on a treaty submitting the controversy to arbitration.[28] Esmé Howard, who had served as British Chargé for a short period before Bryce's arrival, described the atmosphere of the negotiations accurately when he later wrote that Root was "a wonderful man to do business with" and that Root and Bryce "understood each other perfectly." [29] When in early 1909 Root left the cabinet for a seat in the Senate, Bryce reported to Foreign Secretary Grey: "No one regrets his departure from the State Department more than I do. He has done much to bring about an increase of friendly feeling between the United States and Great Britain. . . ." [30]

The outbreak of serious trouble with Japan in the fall of 1906 strongly reinforced Roosevelt's desire for close and friendly relations with Britain. When the San Francisco School Board segregated Japanese school children in October 1906, a series of Japanese-American crises followed which plagued the Roosevelt administration for many months. Roosevelt patched up the school segregation difficulty, but

---

[26] Bryce to Grey, telegram, February 25, 1907, F.O. 115/1434, Public Record Office, London, England.

[27] Bryce to Grey, September 2, 1907, F.O. 115/1436.

[28] Philip C. Jessup, *Elihu Root*, 2 vols. (New York: Dodd, Mead & Co., 1938), II, 89–92.

[29] Esmé Howard, *Theatre of Life*, 2 vols. (London: Hodder & Stoughton, Ltd., 1936), II, 139.

[30] Bryce to Grey, February 6, 1909, F.O. 115/1534.

not before promising the Californians that the flood of Japanese immigration would be checked. It was not until the summer of 1908 that he attained effective implementation of a Gentlemen's Agreement negotiated in 1907 to check immigration; in the interim Japanese-American relations were jarred by successive war scares. The most serious scare came in the summer of 1907 when newspapers throughout Europe and the United States predicted the imminent outbreak of hostilities. The war scares were nothing more than a product of sensational journalism — the Japanese government had not the slightest intention of attacking the United States — but they nevertheless produced uneasiness among American officials. One of the principal reasons for Roosevelt's dispatch of the fleet to the Pacific in 1907 was his desire to silence the Japanese jingo press, an objective that was largely achieved. The sending of the fleet turned out to be the first leg of a world cruise, and by the time the fleet reached the western Pacific, Japanese-American relations had so improved that the fleet received a cordial welcome during a visit at Yokohama.[31]

Throughout the trouble with Japan, Roosevelt sought to work closely with the British, hoping that the London government would exert an influence upon its ally which would help dispel tension. Meanwhile the German Emperor, completely misreading the direction of Roosevelt's policy, sought to turn the Japanese-American troubles to his advantage. Roosevelt was deluged with German intelligence reports on the Japanese fleet, Japanese military readiness, and the possible influx of Japanese reservists into Mexico. The reports which Sternburg relayed from the Foreign Ministry were generally sane and careful analyses — the German Military Attaché at Tokyo, Major von Etsel, consistently reporting no danger of a Japanese attack — but the messages sent by the Kaiser through Ambassador Tower reflected the German ruler's panicky personality and "yellow peril" predelictions. In January 1908 he excitedly sent Roosevelt news of thousands of Japanese laborers in Mexico who were seen after their working hours going through military exercises with staves

---

[31] Raymond A. Esthus, *Theodore Roosevelt and Japan* (Seattle, Wash.: University of Washington Press, 1966), Chapters viii–xv.

in their hands. "Tell the President," he told Tower, "that we estimate that there are in Mexico at present ten thousand regular Japanese soldiers . . . and the Ministers in Peru and Chile report the same
thing from those countries." [32] Roosevelt put no credence in such reports. After receiving one of Major von Etsel's accurate reports
through Sternburg, he remarked to Root, "It helps to correct the
imperial pipe dream forwarded thru Ambassador Tower." [33]

In his memoirs Chancellor Bülow tells of another imperial pipe
dream that never reached Roosevelt's ears. Bülow gives no date for
the episode, but it obviously occurred during 1907 or 1908. It is in-
structive regarding both the Kaiser's personal instability and his ap-
palling naiveté in his relations with Roosevelt. Once when Bülow returned to Berlin after a brief absence, his imperial mentor told him
he had written a "first class" letter to "his friend Roosevelt" which
would really wake him up. When he showed the Chancellor a copy
of the missive, Bülow observed that it contained violent language
against the Japanese and fantastic news of their war preparations. He
told the Kaiser that the communication must not reach Roosevelt, for
the Kaiser must never permit such a weapon against himself to fall
into the President's hands. "But," cried the Kaiser, "Roosevelt is my
friend!" When Bülow explained that "friends" in this sense did not
exist in the world of politics, the Kaiser looked at him very suspicious-
ly. In the end Bülow was able to intercept the dispatch case that
carried the imperial message over the Atlantic; the letter was returned
from New York to Berlin unopened.[34]

In addition to receiving reports from Germany, Roosevelt had oc-
casional talks with Sternburg in which the discussion ranged grandly
over many topics and speculations. In one of these, in November
1907, Roosevelt mentioned the "possibility" of German-American
naval cooperation against Japan,[35] but it would be a mistake to attach
much importance to this remark. Roosevelt was inclined to talk

---

[32] Tower to Roosevelt, January 28, 1908, Roosevelt Papers.

[33] Roosevelt to Root, February 17, 1908, Morison, *Roosevelt Letters, VI,* 946.

[34] Bernhard von Bülow, *Memoirs of Prince von Bülow,* translated by F. A.
Voigt, 4 vols. (Boston: Little, Brown & Co., 1931), *I,* 658–659.

[35] Sternburg to Bülow, November 8, 1907, *Die Grosse Politik, XXV,* 79.

freely — to be precise, carelessly — to his good friend Specky about all sorts of "possibilities." Such conversations, together with Sternburg's inaccurate reports to Berlin, encouraged the German Emperor's belief that Roosevelt would work closely with Germany; but nothing could have been further from reality. In the first place Roosevelt believed the possibility of war with Japan quite remote. Furthermore, the pivot of his policy was not the gaining of German military or naval aid for a war with Japan; it was, rather, the attainment of diplomatic aid from Britain to lessen tension with Japan and avoid a war.

During the crises with Japan, Roosevelt sought relentlessly to attain British diplomatic cooperation vis-à-vis Japan. He wrote long letters to King Edward, Grey, Strachey, Lee, and Spring Rice informing them about the Japanese question and developing the theme that sections of the British Empire and Commonwealth shared the American objection to large-scale Japanese immigration.[36] The British betrayed no eagerness to be drawn into the Japanese-American embroglio, but Roosevelt's chances of securing their aid increased perceptibly when in September 1907 the Anglo-Saxons of Vancouver rioted against the Orientals. Before that incident British leaders were inclined to take a condescending view of the embarrassments of the United States on the Oriental immigration question, but they now became at least dimly aware that they faced similar embarrassments.

When Roosevelt learned of the Vancouver riot, he redoubled his efforts to gain British diplomatic cooperation. The race riot in Vancouver, he wrote to Strachey, "shows once again how like the problems are that our two countries have to meet."[37] British leaders continued to resist Roosevelt's entreaties, but the Dominions soon took steps to support him. In December 1907 Prime Minister Alfred Deakin invited the United States fleet to visit Australia, a move designed to show the mother country that Australia stood with the United States on the Japanese immigration issue.[38] Roosevelt promptly accepted the invi-

---

[36] These letters, too numerous to cite, are found in Morison, *Roosevelt Letters, V, VI.*

[37] Roosevelt to Strachey, September 8, 1907, Morison, *Roosevelt Letters, V,* 787–788.

[38] D. C. Gordon, "Roosevelt's 'Smart Yankee Trick,' " *Pacific Historical Review, XXX* (1961), p. 355.

tation for the same reason.[39] The next month the Canadian Deputy Minister of Labor and Immigration, William L. Mackenzie King, visited Washington to confer with Roosevelt. From this meeting developed Mackenzie King's project to visit London to explain the immigration question to British officials.

In March the Canadian Deputy Minister went to London and convinced British leaders that the British Empire had an Asiatic immigration problem similar to that of the United States. During the course of the Grey–Mackenzie King talks, Grey agreed that if Japan did not observe its Gentlemen's Agreement with Canada, then it must be made clear to the Japanese that their immigration into West Canada must stop. Moreover, said Grey, if the Japanese failed to observe their agreement, the Anglo-Japanese Alliance would not be allowed to hamper Canada in preventing Japanese immigration.[40] After his talks with Mackenzie King, Grey wrote anxiously to Ambassador Bryce that the Pacific slope of Canada was in a high state of excitement and he feared that a suspicion might arise among the people there that Britain would not support them in resisting Japanese immigration. There was, he told Bryce emphatically, no reason whatever for such a suspicion.[41] Arthur Lee reported to Roosevelt that Grey was most anxious to cooperate with the United States. Practically every responsible person agreed, he said, that a complete halt should be called to the immigration of Japanese laborers into the British Empire and America and that, if necessary, the English-speaking countries should cooperate to make the exclusion effective.[42]

Lee was probably overly optimistic about Britain's willingness to cooperate with the United States. Mackenzie King had convinced

---

[39] Oscar King Davis, *Released for Publication: Some Inside Political History of Theodore Roosevelt and His Times, 1898–1918* (Boston: Houghton Mifflin Co., 1925), pp. 87–88.

[40] Private and Secret Memorandum enclosed with Grey to Bryce, March 30, 1908, James Bryce Papers, Bodleian Library, Oxford University, Oxford, England.

[41] Grey to Bryce, March 30, 1908, George M. Trevelyan, *Grey of Fallodon: The Life and Letters of Sir Edward Grey, afterwards Viscount Grey of Fallodon* (Boston and New York: Houghton Mifflin Co., 1937), p. 230.

[42] Lee to Roosevelt, March 31, 1908, Roosevelt Papers.

British leaders only that they also had an Oriental immigration problem, not that the two nations should act together on the problem. Grey was still reluctant to assume a united front with the United States in opposing Japan. His wariness of joint action may even have increased, for during the episode Bryce had expressed the opinion to Grey that Roosevelt's impulsiveness was a danger.[43] The Mackenzie King mission to London nevertheless had been a great gain for Roosevelt, because Britain and the United States, though not ready for joint action, were clearly now on parallel positions vis-à-vis Japanese immigration.

Happily there was soon no need for either joint or parallel action. By the spring of 1908 the Japanese government took increasingly effective steps to implement the Gentlemen's Agreements it had negotiated with Canada and the United States. When the United States immigration statistics for the year 1908 were compiled later, they revealed that more Japanese had left the United States than had entered during that year.

While Roosevelt bent his energies towards closer diplomatic cooperation with Britain, the German Emperor — still misreading the direction of Roosevelt's policy — was attempting to align the United States on the German side of the Anglo-German rivalry. During 1907 the Kaiser watched with increasing alarm the solidification of the alliances and ententes ranged against Germany. Britain's ally Japan signed ententes with France and Russia; then Britain concluded an entente with France's ally Russia. Thus there came into being an anti-German quadruple entente. The creation of this diplomatic combination, which could dominate the Far East and at least balance Germany's Triple Alliance in Europe, was not motivated solely by the desire to check Germany; nevertheless it placed the Germans at a tremendous disadvantage. The Kaiser, with characteristic illusions of grandeur about what he could accomplish, set out to establish a counter grouping to support German interests in the Far East. Thus began his abortive program for a German-Chinese-American alliance.

The Kaiser wanted an alliance or entente with the United States

---

[43] Bryce to Grey, February 6, 1908, Sir Edward Grey Papers, F. O. 800/81, Public Record Office, London, England.

which would have a significant impact in international power politics.[44] Knowing, however, the reluctance of the United States to enter anything like an alliance, he attempted to win Roosevelt's assent by emphasizing a joint declaration in support of the open door policy in China. Roosevelt, on his side, could hardly rebuff categorically a proposal to declare support for what was known to everyone as America's policy; and when he intimated to Sternburg that he might take part in such a joint declaration, Sternburg and the Kaiser deluded themselves into believing that the President would enter a genuine entente or alliance which would align the United States against the British-Japanese-French-Russian combination. The whole matter was thus soon caught up in hopeless confusion.

The mix-up started in November 1907 when Sternburg pressed the Kaiser's scheme upon the President. According to Sternburg's report to Berlin, he urged Roosevelt to make a declaration *of an alliance* supporting the open door, to which Roosevelt replied that such a step might do harm at that time but perhaps the arrival of the United States fleet in the Pacific might be an appropriate time for the declaration of such an alliance.[45] Sternburg's report of this conversation contained the type of inaccuracy typical of his dispatches to Berlin. It is inconceivable that Roosevelt spoke of an *alliance*. Sternburg himself reported less than a month later that Roosevelt declared that an alliance was out of the question.[46] Furthermore, all the evidence on the American side indicates that Roosevelt never deviated from his anti-alliance position throughout his talks with Sternburg. What Roosevelt actually said was that the arrival of the fleet might be an appropriate time for a declaration in support of the open door policy. And even for this modest step he betrayed no enthusiasm. His reply was obviously designed to put Sternburg off politely.

Simultaneously Roosevelt attempted to put the Kaiser off with similar language. He sent a message through Ambassador Tower on November 19, 1907, declaring that he agreed entirely with the Kaiser's position "in the Chinese matter" and that he continued unalterably to favor the preservation of the open door and the maintenance of

---

[44] Tschirschky to Sternburg, September 15, 1907, *Die Grosse Politik, XXV,* 71.
[45] Sternburg to Bülow, November 8, 1907, *Die Grosse Politik, XXV,* 78–79.
[46] Sternburg to Schoen, December 5, 1907, *Die Grosse Politik, XXV,* 80.

China's integrity, but that he did not at the moment believe that anything could be gained by an open statement to that effect.[47] When Roosevelt referred to agreement "in the Chinese matter," he meant, of course, not that he favored the creation of an alliance but that he still supported the open door and the integrity of China. Roosevelt's statement about the time not being opportune was again an attempt to discourage the Kaiser's plans. The German ruler was, however, not easily discouraged. Even after he received Sternburg's report of Roosevelt's statement that an alliance was out of the question, he believed he could draw the United States into an entente. To make the proposal more palatable he proposed to have China take the initiative, thus approaching Roosevelt obliquely. "We could put heavy pressure on Roosevelt through Sternburg," he exclaimed excitedly to Chancellor Bülow, "so that when he gets the proposal he will accept it gladly." [48]

In the succeeding months Roosevelt continued to parry the Kaiser's scheme. Characteristically, while betraying no inclination to act with the Kaiser, he sent him fulsome words about German-American friendship. In a message to the Kaiser in April 1908, he expressed appreciation for the constant friendliness shown by him, and he expressed pleasure at being able to cooperate with him so often.[49]

As it turned out, China was almost as reluctant as Roosevelt to fall in with the Kaiser's plans. China generally desired diplomatic support from any quarter, but the risks of openly aligning itself against the dominant British-Japanese-French-Russian combination could not be taken lightly. In August 1908 the German minister at Peking reported that a Chinese official, Tang Shao-yi, was going to the United States to express appreciation for the remission of Boxer indemnity funds and to pave the way for the German-Chinese-American entente,[50] but actually the Chinese government was still reluctant to proceed with the entente project.

---

[47] Roosevelt to Tower, November 19, 1907, Morison, *Roosevelt Letters, V*, 853.
[48] William II to Bülow, December 30, 1907, *Die Grosse Politik, XXV*, 87–89.
[49] Roosevelt to William II, April 4, 1908, Morison, *Roosevelt Letters, VI*, 993.
[50] Arthur von Rex to the Foreign Office, telegram, August 5, 1908, *Die Grosse Politik, XXV*, 96.

At this juncture of events an extraordinary interview which the Kaiser had given William B. Hale of the New York *Times* became known to Roosevelt, and his reaction to it clearly indicates that he had no intention of entering into an entente with Germany and China. Oscar King Davis of the New York *Times* came to Oyster Bay with a copy of the interview which had taken place in July. Its statements were so explosive that the management of the newspaper wished the President's advice on whether to publish them. The German ruler had railed against England with the most abusive language, characterizing that nation as a traitor to the white race for allying with Japan. He spoke bitterly of King Edward, saying he and all those around him were sunk in ignoble greed and looked at life from a purely stock market standpoint. He even declared that he regarded war between England and Germany as both inevitable and imminent. He went on to declare that he had arranged with the United States to back China against Japan and that a Chinese statesman, Tang Shao-yi, was on the way to Washington to arrange the details.[51] Roosevelt was alarmed at the Kaiser's words and fearful of the harm that would ensue if the interview were published. He therefore convinced the New York *Times* that it should be suppressed. Davis made notes of what Roosevelt said, and his account, published many years later, was as follows:[52]

> This is the funniest thing I have ever known. That Jack of an Emperor talks just as if what he happens to want is already an accomplished fact. He has been at me for over a year to make this kind of an agreement about China, but every time I have replied, "That means a treaty, to which the Senate must consent." . . . This is the first time I have ever heard the name Tang Shao-yi. For at least nine months he — that Jack — has been telling me that a distinguished Chinese official was "on his way" to this country and Germany to settle affairs, but he has never come. I do not know whether this is the man or not. But the policy [the

---

[51] Hale to William C. Reick, July 19 and 24, 1908, quoted in Davis, *Released for Publication,* pp. 81–84; Roosevelt to Root, August 8, 1908, and Roosevelt to Arthur Lee, October 17, 1908, Morison, *Roosevelt Letters, VI,* 1163–1164, 1292–1294.

[52] Davis, *Released for Publication,* pp. 87–88.

open door and the integrity of China], as I have always told the
Emperor, is ours. It has been our policy for seven or eight years,
ever since Hay first enunciated it.
    . . . .
    They say the Emperor and I are alike, and have a great admira-
tion for each other on that account. I do admire him, very much
as I do a grizzly bear.

Tang Shao-yi indeed came to Washington and received the kind of
reception foreshadowed in Roosevelt's remarks to Oscar King Davis.
He arrived on November 30, 1908, just in time to be informed of a
Japanese-American entente one hour before it was announced. By
an exchange of notes between Root and Ambassador Takahira on that
day, Japan and the United States publicly declared it their common
policy to maintain the status quo in the Pacific Ocean area, to respect
each other's territorial possessions in the Pacific, and to support the
integrity of China and the principle of equal opportunity for commerce and industry in China. In undertaking the exchange of notes,
both nations had been motivated almost exclusively by the desire to
silence all the war rumors by issuing an innocuous statement of joint
policy. The event nevertheless constituted a kind of entente, the ne-
gotiators themselves often referring to it as an entente. Whether
Tang even broached the subject of a German-Chinese-American entente in the face of this development is doubtful, but Roosevelt
brought up the subject and made his position clear. He told the Chinese emissary frankly that the United States could not enter any such
combination.[53]

Meanwhile Roosevelt had decided to inform British leaders both of
the contents of the Hale interview and of his heightened apprehensions about the Kaiser. He wrote a long letter to Arthur Lee which he
sent to Henry White by diplomatic pouch. He instructed White to
journey from Paris to London and personally deliver the letter to Lee.
The letter was to be burned immediately after Lee read it, and Lee
was then to inform Grey and Balfour of its contents. Roosevelt's account of the Hale interview in this letter to Lee was complete, includ-

---

[53] Ambassador Johann Heinrich von Bernstorff to the Foreign Office, January
2, 1909, *Die Grosse Politik*, XXV, 97.

ing the Emperor's talk about the imminence of an Anglo-German war. Roosevelt observed that he did not believe the German ruler's statements indicated a settled purpose, but if he was indiscreet enough to talk to a newspaperman in such a fashion, it was barely possible he would be indiscreet enough to act on impulse in a way that would jeopardize the peace. He said that since he had previously argued with British leaders that their fears of Germany were slightly absurd, he felt it incumbent upon himself to say now that he was by no means so confident of this position. As for England, he said he did not believe she had any more intention of acting aggressively than had the United States and he hoped Britain's great navy would be maintained at full efficiency.[54]

Before the letter to Lee arrived at the Paris Embassy, the famous *Daily Telegraph* interview of the Kaiser was published. In this interview, printed on October 28, 1908, the Kaiser described himself as an ardent friend of Britain who had advised the British on how to win the Boer War and was now restraining the German people, whose prevailing sentiment was not friendly to England. The result of the publication was amazement in Britain and a storm of protest in Germany. The British doubted the sincerity of his professed friendship, resented his claim to have helped them win the Boer War, and fully believed his ominous admission that the German people were unfriendly to England. In Germany both Liberals and Socialists strongly criticized his ill-considered utterances and warned of the dangers of his personal rule. The Kaiser was attacked so vigorously that he promised not to talk politics again without his Chancellor's advice.[55] "The Kaiser has come an awful cropper," Roosevelt wrote to his son Kermit.[56]

> He has been a perfect fool, and the German people after standing his folly and bumptiousness for years finally exploded over

---

[54] Roosevelt to Lee, October 17, 1908, Morison, *Roosevelt Letters, VI,* 1292–94.

[55] Sidney B. Fay, *The Origins of the World War,* 2nd ed., 2 vols. in 1 (New York: The Macmillan Co., 1941), *I,* 294–295; Oron J. Hale, *Publicity and Diplomacy, with Special Reference to England and Germany, 1890–1914* (New York, London: D. Appleton-Century Inc., 1940), pp. 313–321.

[56] Roosevelt to Kermit Roosevelt, November 22, 1908, Morison, *Roosevelt Letters, VI,* 1375.

something which was of course bad, but was no worse than scores of similar things he had done before.

After learning of the *Daily Telegraph* interview, Roosevelt decided for several reasons that the letter to Lee about the Hale interview should not be delivered. For one thing, the need was no longer urgent because much of the Hale interview had become public knowledge in England by this time. Also Roosevelt did not wish to risk further inflaming the Anglo-German rivalry at a time when it was already at a high point. When he drafted the letter to Lee several weeks previously, he said in it that he hesitated to write because he did not like to be a Rancy Sniffle, a character in *Georgia Scenes* who was "a stirrer up of strife."[57] Now with the publication of the *Daily Telegraph* interview there was still greater danger that he would fall into that role if his account of the Hale interview reached Lee. Added to these considerations was the fact that the Kaiser had been so humbled by the reaction to the *Daily Telegraph* interview that he could do no immediate mischief against England. "I think that for some time to come," Roosevelt wrote to Ambassador Reid, "the Kaiser will not be a source of serious danger as regards international complications."[58] Roosevelt therefore instructed White not to deliver the letter to Lee, and he told Lee that he would tell him of its contents when he visited England after his planned safari in Africa.[59]

Although Roosevelt drew back from giving the British a full account of the Hale interview in written form, it is likely that he did give its substance orally to Ambassador Bryce under a strict injunction of

---

[57] Roosevelt to Lee, October 17, 1908, Morison, *Roosevelt Letters, VI,* 1292–1294.

[58] Roosevelt to Reid, November 26, 1908, Morison, *Roosevelt Letters, VI,* 1384.

[59] Roosevelt to Lee, November 23, 1908, Morison, *Roosevelt Letters, VI,* 1378–1379. Nevins states that White delivered the letter and burned it on November 28 (*Henry White,* p. 290), but White could not have done this. He left Paris for the United States to vote in the presidential election before Roosevelt's letter to Lee reached the Paris Embassy, and he remained in the United States until early December. On Roosevelt's instructions the letter was sent back to the White House. Adee to Henry Vignaud, telegram, November 4, 1908, S. D. File 2344/43a. Roosevelt saw White on the day the letter was returned to the White House (November 14). He may have given it to White to peruse and then destroy. However this may have been, the letter was not delivered to Lee.

secrecy. On November 18 Bryce sent to Grey a private letter giving an accurate summary of the Hale interview. Bryce explained that the interview had been shown only to the New York *Times* and "one other person," and he hinted that he had been told of the interview by that person. He had been pledged to such secrecy, said Bryce, that he wished Grey not to show his letter to more than the two or three persons to whom its contents ought to be known.[60] As it turned out, the caution was unnecessary. Unknown to Roosevelt and Bryce, the British government already had full knowledge of the Hale interview before the arrival of Bryce's letter. Lord Northcliffe of the London *Times* had a working agreement with the New York *Times* for exchange of information, and he had thereby received an accurate summary of the Hale interview in August. This had been immediately passed on to the Foreign Office.[61] After the arrival of Bryce's letter Grey received an even more complete account of the Hale interview from still another source. The Japanese government had secured the full text of the interview, and in late November it gave a copy to Grey.[62]

The Kaiser's irresponsible utterances in the summer and fall of 1908 completed Roosevelt's disenchantment with the volatile sovereign, but this the Kaiser never realized. Roosevelt continued to ply him with flattery. In December 1908 he thanked him for his "unvarying friendship" and assured him that his personality and position rendered him the most influential and powerful of living men.[63] In view of Roosevelt's consistent leaning toward Britain, it is surprising that the Kaiser accepted these words as sincere and continued to believe that Roosevelt was his special and close friend. There probably was sincerity in some of Roosevelt's words, those characterizing the Emperor as the most influential and powerful of living men, but the inherent

---

[60] Bryce to Grey, November 18, 1908, Grey Papers, F. O. 800/81.

[61] Northcliffe to Sir William Tyrrell, August 21, 1908, F. O. 371/461.

[62] Memorandum to Grey, November 27 and December 21, 1908, Grey Papers, F. O. 800/92. The Japanese copy is in F. O. 371/461 and in the records of the Japanese Foreign Ministry Archives, Telegram Series, *CXII*, 11029–38, microfilm collection, Library of Congress, Washington, D. C.

[63] Roosevelt to William II, December 26, 1908, Morison, *Roosevelt Letters*, *VI*, 1441.

implication that Roosevelt applauded that fact could not have been sincere. World leaders had long viewed the Kaiser's erratic behavior as a danger to peace, and the Hale interview and the *Daily Telegraph* interview brought Roosevelt to fully share this fear. Ambassador Reid reflected the general anxiety when he wrote to Mrs. Roosevelt in November 1908 that the Kaiser's activities constituted the most incredible recklessness in playing with fire.[64]

> From France to Constantinople, and from the Dalmatian coast to St. Petersburg, Europe is at this moment like a powder magazine; and through this magazine goes the short-sighted potentate, striking sparks at almost every movement he makes.

As Roosevelt approached the end of his presidency, he could take reassurance from the fact that the Kaiser's recent humiliation had rendered him at least temporarily powerless to do mischief. The German ruler's position in world politics had reached the weakest point in his reign. His own indiscretions and the solidification of the Entente structure had gravely weakened his position in Europe, and in the Far East his hopes had been shattered by Roosevelt's refusal to go into the alliance scheme. The Root-Takahira exchange of notes had accentuated his discomfiture, for its meaning for the Anglo-American connection was obvious to all. As Roosevelt observed to Arthur Lee, the agreement with Japan was "a good thing as keeping England and America closer together," something he always had "peculiarly at heart."[65]

One of Roosevelt's last acts before leaving the presidency was to make public witness of his friendship for Britain. British leaders often had doubts regarding his pro-British sympathies and questioned why he never made any *public* references to England of a friendly character. The reason was probably discerned by Arthur Lee when he commented to Roosevelt that really good friends "do not need to slobber over each other in public."[66] But now Roosevelt undertook to assure

---

[64] Reid to Mrs. Roosevelt, November, 1908, Cortissoz, *Whitelaw Reid, II,* 377.

[65] Roosevelt to Lee, December 20, 1908, Morison, *Roosevelt Letters, VI,* 1434.

[66] Lee to Roosevelt, January 29, 1909, Roosevelt Papers.

even the doubters. Britain was at this time having difficulties in India, and Roosevelt, in a speech in January 1909, warmly praised the British work there. The British reaction was everything Roosevelt desired. King Edward called in Ambassador Reid to express his appreciation, and Reid reported to Roosevelt that the same feeling was expressed everywhere. Nothing had been done since he had known England, said Reid, that had been so gratefully received or had so encouraged cordial feeling towards the people of the United States.[67]

The month that Roosevelt left the White House, March 1909, witnessed a sharp intensification of the Anglo-German rivalry. On March 12 the cabinet of Prime Minister Herbert Asquith, which had been formed upon the death of Campbell-Bannerman in April 1908, presented to the Parliament a request for construction of six dreadnoughts and two battle cruisers for the next year's program (1909–1910). This call for drastic acceleration in naval construction had been precipitated by the German Naval Bill of 1908 which set the pace of German building at three dreadnoughts and one battle cruiser per year during 1908–1912. This German program, together with the circulation of rumors that the Berlin government was secretly speeding construction still further, caused a serious scare in Britain. Although the Asquith ministry recommended that half of its eight-ship program be approved on a contingency basis pending clarification of the German naval program, the alarm over German construction was so great that by the time Parliament voted approval, the four contingent warships had been made part of the 1909–1910 year's program.[68]

Anglo-American friendship was implicit in the British debate over the naval program. As recently as November 1908 the Asquith ministry had reaffirmed the two-power standard, stating that Britain would maintain a navy stronger than the two next strongest powers, "whatever those powers might be," but in the navy policy of 1909 the United States, which ranked after Germany in naval strength, was specifically omitted from British calculations. During the Japa-

---

[67] Reid to Roosevelt, January 22, 1909, Roosevelt Papers.

[68] Arthur J. Marder, *From Dreadnought to Scapa Flow: The Royal Navy in the Fisher Era, 1904–1919; Volume I, The Road to War, 1904–1914* (London and New York: Oxford University Press, 1961), pp. 151–182.

nese-American troubles in 1907 the Committee of Imperial Defence had held an Anglo-American war to be "not merely the supreme limit of human folly, but also to be so unlikely as to be a contingency against which it is unnecessary to make provision." Britain now adopted this as government policy, establishing a standard of 60 per cent above German strength for future security.[69]

As Britain took measures to meet the German challenge at sea, it became increasingly apparent, even to some German leaders, that the two nations were on a collision course. The German Ambassador to Britain, Count Paul von Wolff-Metternich, told German officials emphatically that it was the German naval program which chiefly poisoned Anglo-German relations.[70] Chancellor Bülow became so disturbed over the Anglo-German thunderstorm which he saw on the horizon that he called a special meeting of German officials to consider the question on June 3, 1909. At this conference Bülow and Metternich, who came from London to take part in the discussion, were unable to convince the Kaiser and Admiral Alfred von Tirpitz that Germany should offer to slow down its building program to achieve an understanding with Britain.[71] Three weeks later Bülow resigned from the Chancellorship and was replaced by Theobald von Bethmann-Hollweg. Although the ostensible reason for Bülow's resignation was an unfavorable vote in the Reichstag on a finance bill, it is probable that the more fundamental motivation for his resignation was his feeling of hopelessness in the face of the opposition of Tirpitz and the Kaiser to a naval understanding with Britain.[72]

The increasing naval rivalry between Britain and Germany brought a renewed emphasis upon the importance of Anglo-American friendship both in Britain and the United States. In Britain former Prime Minister Balfour went so far as to draft a plan for an Anglo-American confederation, though he was realistic enough to know that within the foreseeable future such a proposal could only be a fond hope,

---

[69] Marder, *From Dreadnought to Scapa Flow, I,* 182–185.

[70] Metternich to Bülow, June 2, 1909, *Die Grosse Politik, XXVIII,* 167.

[71] Memorandum of the meeting of June 3, 1909, *Die Grosse Politik, XXVIII,* 168–176.

[72] Fay, *Origins of the World War, I,* 256–259.

not a practical basis for action.[73] Most Americans did not go as far as Balfour in the value they attached to the Anglo-American connection, but many realized the importance of the British navy in the world balance of power. Ambassador Bryce reported from Washington that the recent developments in the naval policies of England and Germany were closely followed in the United States and that the naval expansion of Germany had caused apprehension because of the continuing suspicion that Germany hoped to establish her naval power somewhere on the South American continent. Even American newspapers which had previously been Anglophobe, reported Bryce, were now urging the cultivation of closer ties with Britain.[74]

Amidst the deepening Anglo-German antagonism, Roosevelt's sympathies remained steadfastly on the side of Britain. Since 1906 he had reaffirmed with ever increasing conviction the wisdom of Britain's policy of maintaining naval supremacy, and after he left the White House he continued to state this view. When he toured Europe in 1910, following his safari in Africa, he shared his opinions frankly with leaders at Vienna and Berlin. At the Austrian capital, which he visited first, he declared that German building "was the real cause why other nations were forced into the very great expense attendant upon modern naval preparation." These remarks were relayed by the Austrian government to Berlin, and when Roosevelt reached the German capital himself, he reiterated his views to the Kaiser and to Chancellor Bethmann-Hollweg. In speaking with the Kaiser, he added the comment that if he were an Englishman, he would regard naval supremacy as vital to England and that under no circumstances would he allow mastery of the ocean to be threatened.[75]

When Roosevelt reached England he told Arthur Lee much of what he had said and learned on the continent, and he warned that Germany might very possibly — whether probably or not he could not

[73] Kenneth Young, Arthur James Balfour: The Happy Life of the Politician, Prime Minister, Statesman, and Philosopher, 1848–1930 (London: G. Bell & Sons, 1963), pp. 277–284.

[74] Bryce to Grey, April 27, 1909, F. O. 115/1534.

[75] Roosevelt to Trevelyan, October 1, 1911, Morison, Roosevelt Letters, VII, 378–379, 396, 398.

say — strike at England if it thought the chance favorable.[76] After
his return to the United States he sent Trevelyan a long account of
what he told the Germans and his own analysis of the German danger. He was inclined to believe that the Kaiser himself had no conscious intention to use his navy for an attack on England, but he was
convinced that Germany wished to have a navy so strong that it
could assume the same arrogant tone with England that it assumed
toward France. This Roosevelt feared would eventually bring war. If
Germany had a navy as strong as that of Britain, even though the
Kaiser did not intend to use it for the destruction of Britain, incidents
would likely occur which might make him so use it.[77]

Thus Roosevelt came to essentially the same conclusion as that
reached by Eyre Crowe in his famous Foreign Office memorandum of
January 1, 1907. It did not matter whether German policy consciously
intended the destruction of Britain. Germany could not be permitted
to build a navy powerful enough to accomplish Britain's destruction.
As the world headed towards the holocaust of World War I, Roosevelt was convinced that on the crucial naval question Grey, Crowe,
and other British leaders were following the only policy compatible
with Britain's security.

---

[76] Roosevelt to Lee, August 22, 1914, Morison, *Roosevelt Letters, VII,* 812.
[77] Roosevelt to Trevelyan, October 1, 1911, Morison, *Roosevelt Letters, VII,*
378–379, 396, 398.

Rivalries in East Asia

7

In the years that followed the Russo-Japanese War, the focal point of East Asian international rivalries was Manchuria. Although the Portsmouth Peace Conference brought a cessation of fighting in that cradle of conflict, it did not end the many rivalries there. A host of contending forces continued to tug and pull at the warped fabric of Chinese sovereignty in Manchuria as the powers sought to protect and further their varied strategic, political, or economic interests.

The Sino-Japanese clash of interests emerged as the most fundamental of the postwar rivalries. Manchuria, after all, was Chinese territory, and with Russia temporarily weakened in the Far East, it was Japan which sought most vigorously to defend and develop its interests there. As a result of the Russo-Japanese War, Japan had secured the naval base at Port Arthur and the trunk-line railroad stretching from Changchun to Port Arthur. In addition it had secured from China in 1905 certain timber rights in Manchuria and the right to link the Korean railways with the South Manchuria Railway. Japan did not have a perfect sphere of influence in South Manchuria, as Germany had in Shantung Province with its exclusive right to invest capital, but Japan's interests were so substantial that it could be anticipated that it would seek to dominate capital investment in the area. In 1907 Japan strengthened its claim to a sphere of influence by treaties with France and Russia which, by implication, recognized a Japanese political interest in South Manchuria that went beyond the economic rights Japan could claim by its treaties with China. That Japan's ally Britain would also accord Japan a sphere of influence in South Manchuria virtually went without saying. Thus the stage was set for a protracted Sino-Japanese struggle as China sought to preserve as much of its sovereignty and administrative integrity as possible in the face of Japan's growing interests in South Manchuria.

The importance of the Sino-Japanese rivalry in Manchuria was not as apparent during Roosevelt's presidency as it became later. During 1906–1909 other rivalries often caused more thunder to roll across the Manchurian plains. The Sino-Russian clash of interests brought the sharpest diplomatic controversy when Russia in 1907 and 1908 sought to assert sovereignty over large Chinese cities along the line of the Russian-owned Chinese Eastern Railway in North Manchuria. That controversy brought into play still another rivalry in Manchuria, that between the sphere-holding powers, Russia and Japan, and the western commercial powers, principally the United States and Britain. Although the American and British interests related almost exclusively to trade, those interests were greatly affected by the political, economic, and strategic rivalries of the other countries.

The conflict of interest between the sphere-holding powers and the commercial powers was the rivalry that most directly affected the United States; yet Roosevelt showed little interest in the question of the open door for commerce in postwar Manchuria. Before the war, when Russia threatened American commercial activity in Manchuria, he went so far as to speculate with Hay about using force against Russia, but when in 1905–1906 Japan blocked commercial access to South Manchuria for many months while it evacuated Japanese military forces, he betrayed no concern. The United States sent protests to Tokyo, but these embodied the views and anxieties of Secretary Root rather than those of the President. During the Russo-Japanese War, Roosevelt had received from Japan a pledge to observe the open door in Manchuria, and he apparently felt reasonably sure that the commitment would be honored once the bulk of Japanese military forces were withdrawn. Fortunately his confidence was soon shown to be justified. In the summer of 1906 most commercial centers in South Manchuria were opened to foreign interests, and in the subsequent months the Japanese military evacuation was carried out ahead of the eighteen-month schedule provided for in the Portsmouth Treaty. Concurrently American diplomats in the Far East, including W. W. Rockhill at Peking and Luke E. Wright at Tokyo, reported to Washington that Japan was in fact observing the open door for commerce.[1]

Even if Japan had not observed the open door for commerce, it is doubtful that the President would have undertaken a vigorous assertion of American trading rights, for he had great respect for Japan's strategic interests in South Manchuria. To Roosevelt the long-standing Russo-Japanese conflict of interests in Manchuria was still the most fundamental. Despite the Portsmouth Treaty and the later entente of 1907 in which the two powers recognized each other's sphere of influence, Roosevelt was convinced that the basic strategic rivalry remained. He believed that Japan, therefore, had an interest in South Manchuria which transcended those of the western commercial powers, for it involved Japan's national security. If in the course of defending its strategic interest Japan encroached upon the economic interests of other nations, Roosevelt was inclined to view such actions sympathetically. Even more important, his respect for the Japanese strategic interest in South Manchuria was so great that it led him to give little more than lip service to the concept of China's sovereignty there.

Roosevelt's regard for Japan's strategic interest was repeatedly manifested both during and after the Russo-Japanese War. In June 1904 he stated to Japanese Minister Takahira and Special Envoy Kaneko that Japan should have a "paramount interest" in what surrounded the Yellow Sea.[2] A year later he told Takahira that Japan had won "dominance in Manchuria,"[3] a remark that showed scant respect for China's sovereignty. During the Portsmouth Peace Conference he assured the Japanese government through Kaneko that it had attained

---

[1] Wright to Root, August 11, 1906, United States, Department of State, *Papers Relating to the Foreign Relations of the United States, 1906,* 2 vols. (Washington, D. C.: Government Printing Office, 1909), *I,* 217–218; Rockhill to Root, October 11, 1906, *Foreign Relations, 1906, I,* 225–226.

[2] Roosevelt to Spring Rice, June 13, 1904, Elting E. Morison (ed.), *The Letters of Theodore Roosevelt,* 8 vols. (Cambridge, Mass.: Harvard University Press, 1951–1954), *IV,* 830.

[3] Roosevelt to Lodge, June 16, 1905, Morison, *Roosevelt Letters, IV,* 1230.

"control" of Manchuria and Korea.[4] The day after the signing of the Portsmouth Treaty he wrote to Colonel George Harvey that Japan had secured control of Manchuria and Korea.[5] For Roosevelt to speak of Japan's "control" of Manchuria in the same sense as Japanese control of Korea revealed an extraordinary indifference to China's sovereignty in Manchuria. Roosevelt favored the restoration of Manchuria to Chinese administrative control after the war, and this was provided for in the Portsmouth Treaty. But in view of what Roosevelt regarded as China's contemptible military weakness and administrative incapacity, he apparently believed that Chinese sovereignty over the area would be more nominal than real.

In the years following the Russo-Japanese War, Roosevelt's respect for Japan's strategic interest in South Manchuria did not diminish. On the contrary, the outbreak of trouble with Japan in 1906 over mistreatment of Japanese in California made him even more inclined to tread warily in any matter affecting Japan's position in Manchuria. His continuing scant regard for China's sovereignty in Manchuria was apparent in 1908 when Japan suggested a Japanese-American entente, the proposal which led to the Root-Takahira exchange of notes. At that time he told Takahira that in matters relating to China's sovereignty he was willing to treat Manchuria differently from the rest of China.[6] Two years later he sent a letter to his successor, President Taft, that gives the deepest insight into his attitude toward Japan. He said that Japan's powers, interests, and intentions in Manchuria must be judged "on the actual facts of the case, and not be mere study of treaties."[7] Thus Roosevelt recognized in his own mind a Japanese interest in Manchuria that went beyond those rights which were legally established by treaties.

---

[4] Roosevelt to Kaneko, August 23, 1905, Morison, *Roosevelt Letters, IV,* 1312–1313.

[5] Roosevelt to Harvey, September 6, 1905, Theodore Roosevelt Papers, Library of Congress, Washington, D. C.

[6] Takahira to Komura, September 6, 1908, Telegram, Series, *CX,* 7699–7704, Japanese Ministry of Foreign Affairs Archives, microfilm collection, Library of Congress, Washington, D. C.

[7] Roosevelt to Taft, December 8, 1910, Morison, *Roosevelt Letters, VII,* 180–181.

It is ironic that during the Roosevelt administration the highest diplomatic official of the United States in Manchuria, the Consul General at Mukden, pursued policies and programs which ran directly counter to Roosevelt's views. In the summer of 1906 Willard Straight was appointed Consul General at Mukden, and soon after his arrival at his post he embarked upon an anti-Japanese crusade which endangered not only Japan's economic interests but her strategic position as well. Straight was a young idealist who felt a personal commitment to defend helpless China from what he regarded as the dragon of Japanese imperialism. He grudgingly conceded that Japan was observing the open door for ordinary commerce in South Manchuria,[8] which was all that John Hay had requested in his famous open door notes, but Straight wanted equal opportunity for capital investment as well. He contemplated destroying the Japanese sphere of influence in South Manchuria by pumping into that area the superior capital resources of the United States.

Unfortunately for Straight, his biggest project collapsed because of the financial panic in the United States in 1907. He hoped to set up a Manchuria Bank financed by American capital which would dominate investment enterprise in Manchuria. When he sought to interest Edward H. Harriman in the undertaking, however, the American railroad mogul rejected the proposal because of the uncertain financial conditions on Wall Street.[9] With the failure of this project Straight turned his attention to a scheme being concocted by his British friends J. O. P. Bland and Lord ffrench: the Hsinmintun-Fakumen railway project. This undertaking was designed to drive to the wall Japan's principal investment enterprise in Manchuria, the South Manchuria Railway, by constructing a new line parallel to the Japanese line. In November 1907 Lord ffrench signed a contract with Chinese officials for the construction of a railway from Hsinmintun, the northern terminus of China's railway system, northward to Fakumen. A secret

---

[8] Straight to Edwin Denby, December 3, 1907, Willard Straight Papers, Albert R. Mann Library, Cornell University, Ithaca, New York.

[9] Herbert Croly, *Willard Straight* (New York: The Macmillan Co., 1924), pp. 241–242; Straight diary, August 7, 1907, and Harriman to Straight, October 5, 1907, Straight Papers.

agreement was signed at the same time for the extension of the line to Tsitsihar in northern Manchuria. Lord ffrench was visiting Straight at the time the contract was signed, and they joyfully celebrated what they knew was a direct blow at Japan.[10] Straight confided to Third Assistant Secretary of State Huntington Wilson, his friend at the State Department who shared his anti-Japanese views, that the new line would seriously compete with the Japanese railroad and that it would even threaten the Japanese strategic position by placing a splendid line along the Japanese flank within easy reach of the Russians.[11]

The railway project was destined to fail just as decisively as did the Manchurian Bank scheme. Japan revealed that in 1905 China had signed an agreement not to build any line parallel to the SMR, whereupon the British government withdrew diplomatic support from Pauling and Company, the British firm that was to build the line.[12] Straight was discouraged, but he doggedly went on with other projects to counter the Japanese in Manchuria until the State Department recalled him to Washington in the summer of 1908.

Roosevelt and Straight were at opposite poles in their attitude toward Manchuria. It is inconceivable that Roosevelt would have knowingly allowed an American diplomat to wage an anti-Japanese crusade in South Manchuria. He was obviously unaware of Straight's views and activities. The President kept a keen eye on the Japanese troubles in the United States, but in the period following the Russo-Japanese War he was amazingly uninformed about developments in East Asia. Rockhill, the Minister at Peking, discerned at least to some extent the character of Straight's program, and he may have informed Root of the Consul General's activities when he visited Washington in January 1908. But if he did, the information apparently did not reach Roosevelt's ears.

However much Root knew of Straight's crusade, it would have disturbed him less than Roosevelt, for the Secretary of State's attitude

---

[10] Straight diary, November 5, 1907, and Straight to Henry Schoelkopf, March 22, 1908, Straight Papers.

[11] Straight to Wilson, January 31, 1908, Straight Papers.

[12] Raymond A. Esthus, *Theodore Roosevelt and Japan* (Seattle, Wash.: University of Washington Press, 1966), pp. 238–240.

toward Manchurian affairs differed from that of the President. Root did not favor any attack on Japan's legally established rights in Manchuria, as Straight advocated, but neither did he favor giving the Japanese a free hand to secure more rights or to interpret existing treaty rights in a manner which did violence to China's sovereignty. Roosevelt, the proponent of *Realpolitik,* believed that Japan's rights and interests in Manchuria must be judged on the actual facts, not by "mere study of treaties." Root, the student of international law, believed that Japan's rights and interests must be judged precisely by the study of treaties. Furthermore, in studying the treaties Root gave great weight to the concept of China's national sovereignty, something Roosevelt certainly did not do.

Root's attitude toward Manchurian affairs was clearly revealed when in 1908 he became deeply involved in the Russo-Chinese controversy over Russian administrative rights in the zone of the Russian-owned Chinese Eastern Railway. Under the Russo-Chinese contract of 1896,[13] Russia claimed exclusive administrative rights in the railway zone which stretched across Manchuria, and in late 1907 the St. Petersburg government drafted plans for a Russian municipal government at the city of Harbin. At the core of the dispute was the question of China's sovereignty in Manchuria, and during the course of the controversy Root became the principal champion of China's integrity. Technically he was only supporting the rights of the United States and other western commercial powers against an erroneous interpretation of treaty rights by a sphere-holding power, but this placed him in the forefront of the fight to defend China's sovereignty in Manchuria.

The United States was first drawn into the Russo-Chinese controversy when in February 1908 Russia objected to the support given to China by the United States Consul at Harbin, Fred D. Fisher.[14] Root was not long in perceiving that the issue was fraught with great

---

[13] John V. A. MacMurray, *Treaties and Agreements with and concerning China, 1894–1919,* 2 vols. (London and New York: Oxford University Press, 1921), *I,* 74–77.

[14] Imperial Russian Embassy to the Department of State, February 4, 1908, United States, Department of State, *Papers Relating to the Foreign Relations of the United States, 1910* (Washington, D. C.: Government Printing Office, 1915), p. 202.

significance. Chargé Henry P. Fletcher, when asked for a report on the dispute, pointed out that if the right of municipal administration were conceded to the Russians at Harbin, the Japanese, having succeeded to the rights of the Chinese Eastern Railway Company in South Manchuria, would claim the same privileges there.[15] William Phillips, the Chief of the Division of Far Eastern Affairs, agreed. He warned Root that if the United States recognized an absolute Russian administration at Harbin, it would constitute formal acquiescence in the principle of the erection by Russia and Japan of large cities within Manchuria wholly independent of China. "The integrity of China," said Phillips, "would be at an end." [16] Root quickly concluded that Fletcher and Phillips were right. On March 10 he jotted down a succinct observation which was to characterize his policy throughout the controversy: "We cannot recognize this attempt to exclude Chinese sovereignty." [17]

Throughout 1908 in notes to St. Petersburg Root quietly but firmly opposed the Russian claim.[18] Concurrently he took the lead in marshalling the other western treaty powers in defense of China's sovereignty. Berlin pledged support,[19] but the London government, having recently concluded its entente with St. Petersburg, at first gave only half-hearted support.[20] Root finally wrung from Sir Edward Grey, however, a commitment to use British influence at both St. Petersburg and Tokyo.[21] In the meantime in talks with the Japanese Ambassador at Washington, Root sought to dissuade Japan from

---

[15] Fletcher to Root, February 14, 1908, S. D. File 4002/36–42, Records of the Department of State, National Archives, Washington D. C.

[16] Memorandum by Phillips, March 6, 1908, S. D. File 4002/26.

[17] Note by Root, March 10, 1908, S. D. File 4002/24–26.

[18] Root to Chargé Kroupensky, July 2, 1908, and Root to Rosen, December 29, 1908, Foreign Relations, 1910, pp. 206–208.

[19] Hatzfeldt to Bacon, May 30, 1908, S. D. File 4002/103–104; Phillips to Rockhill, June 3, 1908, William W. Rockhill Papers; Houghton Library, Harvard University, Cambridge, Massachusetts.

[20] Root to Reid, April 11, May 22 and 30, 1908, Reid to Root, April 28 (telegram) and May 5, 1908, Whitelaw Reid Papers, Library of Congress, Washington, D. C.

[21] Reid to Root, telegrams, June 12, 18, and 24, S. D. File 4002/111–114; Reid to Root, June 15 and 30, 1908, Reid Papers.

supporting Russia or from advancing a similar claim to governmental authority in the zone of the South Manchuria Railway.[22]

Root was reluctant to become so deeply involved in the Manchurian rivalry; yet he felt he had to uphold United States treaty rights and, at the same time, shield China from a serious blow to its integrity. In September 1908 Phillips, in a letter to Rockhill, accurately summed up Root's attitude:[23]

> I do not think that the Department intends to have trouble in Manchuria, either with Russia or Japan. The Secretary is especially anxious not to become embroiled in little incidents with either of those two powers; but when Russia makes a demand that we relinquish our extraterritorial rights in Harbin and on all railway property, in favor of Russia, we can not very well agree to her proposal without hitting China pretty hard.

Reluctant though he was to be involved in a dispute with the sphere-holding powers, Root continued to lead the struggle for China's sovereignty in Manchuria until he left the Secretaryship of State for the Senate in January 1909. In May 1909 his policy achieved some success when a Russo-Chinese agreement was signed which recognized the sovereignty of China in the railway zone as a fundamental principle.[24]

In the fight to preserve Chinese sovereignty in Manchuria in 1908–1909 Roosevelt took no part. Root may have consulted him from time to time, but the records do not give even a hint that Roosevelt had any knowledge of the Harbin issue. If he did, he took no interest in the matter and exerted no perceptible influence. The only recorded indication of Roosevelt's attitude in 1908 is his remark to Ambassador Takahira that he was willing to treat Manchuria differently from the rest of China[25] — a remark which was in line with his often manifested disregard for China's sovereignty in Manchuria, but which was clearly out of line with Root's policy.

When Japan in October 1908 proposed an entente with the United

---

[22] Root to Reid, May 22, 1908, Reid Papers.

[23] Phillips to Rockhill, September 19, 1908, Rockhill Papers.

[24] Rockhill to Secretary of State Philander C. Knox, May 14, 1909, S. D. File 4002/186.

[25] Takahira to Komura, September 6, 1908, Telegram Series, *CX*, 7699–7704.

States, Roosevelt pursued a similar hands-off attitude. The negotiations were left entirely to Root, and Roosevelt allowed Root's attitude to prevail. Although the entente project was undertaken for the purpose of stilling war rumors and was thus in the nature of an innocuous publicity undertaking, the question of China's integrity could not very well be skirted in the formulation of a joint policy statement. Root and Takahira agreed to leave the Harbin dispute out of the negotiations, but Root nevertheless insisted upon the inclusion of a statement in support of China's integrity which was applicable to Manchuria and the remainder of China alike. The Japanese secured a phraseology which they thought would leave them somewhat more leeway in Manchuria than that proposed by Root, but so far as the records indicate, Root had no knowledge of the Japanese motivation in proposing the change. Instead of declaring their common policy to maintain the integrity and administrative entity of China, as originally proposed by Root, the final draft of the exchange of notes declared the desire to assure the independence and integrity of the Chinese Empire. Such a statement supporting China's integrity was at least a limited victory for Root in the Harbin issue, and he was content otherwise to leave that question out of the negotiations. Japan thus far had not made a claim to exclusive jurisdiction in the railway zone in South Manchuria, as Russia had made in the north, and the Root-Takahira exchange of notes did not specifically forestall Tokyo from asserting such a claim in the future. At the same time, the United States was left free to oppose such a claim. Moreover, Root's attitude in the Harbin dispute and in the Root-Takahira negotiations had made it clear to Japan that if Root were formulating United States policy, the United States would oppose resolutely such a claim by Japan.[26]

Root conferred with Roosevelt from time to time during the negotiations with Takahira, but it was clearly the Root attitude that predominated in the formulation of United States policy. If Japan had made a vigorous demand for a free hand in Manchuria — that is, prior United States approval for whatever claims Japan might make in South Manchuria in the future — the differences in attitude be-

[26] The Root-Takahira negotiations are recounted in Esthus, *Theodore Roosevelt and Japan*, Ch. xvi.

145

tween the President and the Secretary of State would doubtless have been brought to the surface, and probably resolved in favor of the President and the Japanese. But Japan made no such demand and even agreed to the inclusion of the clause supporting China's integrity. Thus Root emerged from the negotiations of 1908 with his policy intact. That policy, simply stated, was to recognize Japan's legally established rights in Manchuria, to avoid an aggressive attack on those rights, but to resist any interpretation of those treaty rights which appeared unreasonable or which did further violence to China's sovereignty.

When the Taft administration took over the formulation of America's East Asian policy, it quickly scrapped Root's policy — not in favor of Roosevelt's attitude of beneficence toward Japan, but in favor of Straight's anti-Japanese crusade. Straight himself became the agent of the American banking group which was formed to invest in China, and Huntington Wilson, who was strongly anti-Japanese, was named First Assistant Secretary of State. Straight was soon pushing another plan to parallel the Japanese-owned South Manchuria Railway, and Philander C. Knox, the Secretary of State, embarked upon a concerted program to counter the Japanese and Russians in Manchuria. In 1909 Knox went so far as to propose the placing of all Manchurian railways under international control.[27]

The schemes of Straight and Knox were destined to founder on the rock of the Anglo-Japanese Alliance, but not before stirring the ire of both the Japanese and Roosevelt. The ex-President was appalled at the Taft administration's China policy. He sent several letters to Taft in which he succinctly stated the premises which had dominated his ideas about Manchuria since the Russo-Japanese War. On December 8, 1910, he voiced the view, which has already been noted, that Japan's powers, interests, and intentions in Manchuria must be judged on the actual facts of the case, not by mere study of treaties.[28] Two weeks later he expounded his views to Taft at greater length.

---

[27] Charles Vevier, *The United States and China, 1906–1913* (New Brunswick, N. J.: Rutgers University Press, 1955), pp. 124–170.

[28] Roosevelt to Taft, December 8, 1910, Morison, *Roosevelt Letters, VII*, 180–181.

Our vital interest is to keep the Japanese out of our country, and at the same time to preserve the good will of Japan. The vital interest of the Japanese, on the other hand, is in Manchuria and Korea. It is therefore peculiarly to our interest not to take any steps as regards Manchuria which will give the Japanese cause to feel, with or without reason, that we are hostile to them, or a menace — in however slight a degree — to their interests.

How vital Manchuria was to Japan and how impossible it was for her to submit to outside interference, he went on to say, could be deduced from the fact that she was laying down triple lines of track from Port Arthur to Mukden as an answer to the double tracking of the Siberian railway by the Russians. He was convinced that however friendly the superficial relations of Russia and Japan might be, Japan knew perfectly well that at some time in the future Russia would "wish to play a game of bowls for the prize she lost in their last contest." [29]

Roosevelt's words were heeded neither by Taft nor his successors in the White House. The anti-Japanese policy of Willard Straight set the tone of future American policy — though, strangely, United States policy at times veered dizzily to the Roosevelt position, as in the Lansing-Ishii exchange of notes in 1917 which recognized that Japan had special interests in China based upon propinquity. Root's policy, which occupied a reasonable and judicious middle ground between the Roosevelt and Straight extremes, was lost from sight. The later policy makers at Washington usually condemned Root and Roosevelt as being equally pro-Japanese.

Unfortunately, Root himself in later years made statements which blurred the distinction between his attitude and Roosevelt's. At the Far Eastern sessions of the Washington Conference of 1921–1922 he suggested treating China proper and the "outlying districts" of China separately with regard to the open door and the integrity of China.[30] Root, whose knowledge of Chinese geography left something to be

---

[29] Roosevelt to Taft, December 22, 1910, Morison, *Roosevelt Letters, VII*, 189–191.

[30] Minutes of the Second Meeting of the Committee on Pacific and Far Eastern Questions, November 19, 1921, United States, Department of State, *Conference on the Limitation of Armament* (Washington, D. C.: Government Printing Office, 1922), p. 882.

desired, probably did not intend to include Manchuria among the outlying districts, but his obscure statement left him open to the suspicion that he was as pro-Japanese as Roosevelt had been. His inclusion of a clause in the Nine Power Treaty pledging the signatories not to countenance action inimical to the security of friendly states also seemed to substantiate that he was unduly solicitous of the Japanese position in Manchuria.[31] On the other hand, Root authored the most important check on Japan's actions contained in the Nine Power Treaty, that which pledged the signatories to seek no further rights designed to create spheres of influence.[32] This position, which avoided attacking existing treaty rights but resisted the gaining of new rights, was precisely in line with the policy Root had followed while Secretary of State.[33]

Root's dominant role in the formulation of America's East Asian policy in the years 1906–1908 underscores the fact that after the Portsmouth Peace Conference Roosevelt became more concerned about the international rivalries in Europe than those in East Asia. The attention he gave Far Eastern questions was devoted almost exclusively to the Japanese troubles in California and the Japanese-

---

[31] Sadao Asada, "Japan's 'Special Interests' and the Washington Conference, 1921–22," *American Historical Review,* LXVII (1961–62) p. 67. This article is somewhat confusing in that it does not distinguish between Japan's special interests in the sense of legally established treaty rights and special interests which she claimed by reason of propinquity.

[32] Minutes of the Twenty-third Meeting of the Committee on Pacific and Far Eastern Questions, January 21, 1922, *Conference on the Limitation of Armament,* p. 1340.

[33] By 1931 when Japan was seizing Manchuria, Root may have become even more pro-Japanese than Roosevelt had been, though the evidence is not entirely convincing. Secretary of State Henry L. Stimson recorded in his diary on November 14, 1931: "Allen Klots brought me back interesting news from Mr. Root. Rather to my surprise Mr. Root is more sympathetic with Japan than with China; and he is very fearful lest we do not recognize her real claims to Manchuria." Quoted in Richard N. Current, *Secretary Stimson: A Study in Statecraft* (New Brunswick, N. J.: Rutgers University Press, 1954), p. 87. This is, however, third-hand information coming from Root via Klots and Stimson, and it is so far out of line with the policy Root pursued while Secretary of State that it is suspect. What Root may have said to Klots was that he hoped the United States would recognize Japan's *rights in* Manchuria, not her *claims to* Manchuria.

American crises resulting therefrom, and he betrayed virtually no interest in the rivalries in East Asia. Still, he had some influence upon Root's handling of Manchurian affairs. Root well knew, and shared to an extent, Roosevelt's desire not to antagonize Japan needlessly over East Asian matters in the face of the difficulties over Japanese immigration. This, plus Roosevelt's high regard for Japan's strategic interests in Manchuria, obviously placed limits upon Root's freedom of action in pursuing his policy of defending the open door and the integrity of China. But these limits were vague, and fortunately for all concerned, Japan did not force matters to a point where they became decisive in the determination of American policy.

Roosevelt's preoccupation with the European rivalry resulted from his belief that the Anglo-German antagonism was fraught with more peril to world peace than any Asian rivalry or even the Japanese-American friction over the immigration problem. The immigration issue and the related matter of discrimination against Japanese in California caused Roosevelt more bother and concern than any other question during his presidency, but still he ranked it second to the Anglo-German rivalry as a source of future conflict. When he visited Europe in 1910 he discovered that many Europeans anticipated two wars — one between Japan and the United States, one between Britain and Germany. In discussing this theory with Austrian Prime Minister Richard von Bienerth, he declared that he did not believe war would ever come between Japan and the United States, but he expressed no such confidence about the possibility of an Anglo-German war.[34] What Roosevelt learned at Berlin did not give him any reassurance. Although the Kaiser insisted that he "ADORED ENGLAND!" Roosevelt remained unconvinced. When he reached England, as has been noted, he warned Arthur Lee that Germany might very possibly strike at England if it thought the chance favorable.[35]

By the fall of 1911 Roosevelt's anti-German views — which were to be so vehemently expressed after the outbreak of World War I —

[34] Roosevelt to Trevelyan, October 1, 1911, Morison, *Roosevelt Letters, VII*, 377.

[35] Roosevelt to Lee, August 22, 1914, Morison, *Roosevelt Letters, VII*, 812.

were already fully formed. Germany was the chief danger to peace, not Japan. Japan's eyes were fixed on the mainland of Asia, he observed to Francis V. Greene in March, 1911. Its concern was so predominantly with Russia and China that it was not likely that it would go to war with the United States.[36] In September 1911 his continuing anxiety over the Anglo-German rivalry was evident when he told Arthur Lee emphatically that Britain was absolutely right in keeping up its war power.[37] That Roosevelt considered this vital not only to Britain but to the United States as well was apparent in a letter he wrote the next month to his brother-in-law, Rear Admiral William S. Cowles. In it he declared: "If Germany should ever overthrow England and establish the supremacy in Europe she aims at, she will be almost certain to want to try her hand in America." [38] This view was the logical culmination of the whole direction of Roosevelt's thoughts from 1906 to 1911. Europe was still the fulcrum of international diplomacy, and in the game of world politics the most important issue was whether Britain would meet and triumph over an aggressive Germany.

---

[36] Roosevelt to Greene, March 7, 1911, Morison, *Roosevelt Letters, VII,* 239.

[37] Roosevelt to Lee, September 25, 1911, Morison, *Roosevelt Letters, VII,* 347.

[38] Roosevelt to Cowles, October 27, 1911, Morison, *Roosevelt Letters, VII,* 423.

Bibliography

Unpublished Materials
I. PRIVATE PAPERS
Arthur James Balfour Papers, British Museum.

James Bryce Papers, Bodleian Library, Oxford University.

Edward Grey Papers, Public Record Office.

John Hay Papers, Library of Congress.

Henry Lansdowne Papers, Public Record Office.

George von Lengerke Meyer Papers, Library of Congress.

Whitelaw Reid Papers, Library of Congress.

William Woodville Rockhill Papers, Houghton Library, Harvard University.

Theodore Roosevelt Papers, Library of Congress.

Elihu Root Papers, Library of Congress.

Cecil Spring Rice Papers, custody of Lady Elizabeth Arthur, London, England.

Willard Straight Papers, Albert R. Mann Library, Cornell University.

Henry White Papers, Library of Congress.

II. OFFICIAL RECORDS
Great Britain, Public Record Office.
    F.O. 5 General Correspondence: United States.
    F.O. 115 Embassy and Consular Archives: United States.
    F.O. 371 General Political Correspondence.
    F.O. 414 Confidential Print: North America.
    F.O. 425 Confidential Print: Northern and Western Europe.
    F.O. 800 Private Collections.

Japan, Ministry of Foreign Affairs Archives, Microfilm Collection, Library of Congress.
    Telegram Series, 1902–1909, reels 32-115.
    PVM 9-55 Collection of Cabinet Decisions (Kakugo Kettei-sho shūroku), reels P14-P15.

United States, National Archives.
　RG 59: General Records of the Department of State.

Published Materials

I. OFFICIAL DOCUMENTS

Dugdale, E. T. S. *German Diplomatic Documents, 1871–1914,* 4 vols. (London: Methuen & Co., 1928–1931).

France, Ministere des Affaires Etrangères. *Documents Diplomatique Francais (1871–1914),* 2nd series, 1901–1911 (Paris: Imprimerie National, 1930–1955).

Germany, Auswärtiges Amt. *Die Grosse Politik der Europäischen Kabinette, 1871–1914,* 40 vols. (Berlin: Deutsche verlagsgesellschaft für politik und geschichte, 1922–1927).

Gooch, G. P., and Harold Temperley. *British Documents on the Origins of the War, 1898–1914,* 11 vols. (London: His Majesty's Stationery Office, 1926–1938).

Japan, Gaimusho. *Komura Gaikoshi,* 2 vols. (Tokyo: Gaimusho, 1953).

MacMurray, John V. A. *Treaties and Agreements With and Concerning China, 1894–1919,* 2 vols. (London and New York: Oxford University Press, 1921).

Russia, Ministerstovo inostrannykh del. *Sbornik diplomaticheskikh dokumentov kasaiushchikhsia peregovorov mezhdu Rossiei i Iaponiei o zakliuchenii mirnogo dogovora, 24 maia-3 oktiabria, 1905* (St. Petersburg, 1906).

United States, Department of State. *Papers Relating to the Foreign Relations of the United States* (Washington: Government Printing Office, 1861–).

II. CORRESPONDENCE

Abbott, Lawrence F., (ed.) *The Letters of Archie Butt, Personal Aide to President Roosevelt* (Garden City, N. Y.: Doubleday, Page & Co., 1924).

Gwynn, Stephen. *The Letters and Friendships of Sir Cecil Spring Rice: A Record,* 2 vols. (Boston and New York: Houghton Mifflin Co., 1929).

Lodge, Henry Cabot. *Selections from the Correspondence of Theodore Roosevelt and Henry Cabot Lodge, 1884–1918,* 2 vols. (New York: Charles Scribner's Sons, 1925).

Morison, Elting E., (ed.) *The Letters of Theodore Roosevelt,* 8 vols. (Cambridge: Harvard University Press, 1951–1954).

Rich, Norman, and M. H. Fisher (eds.) *The Holstein Papers,* 4 vols. (Cambridge, England: Cambridge University Press, 1955–1963).

III. MEMOIRS AND DIARIES

Bülow, Bernhard von. *Memoirs of Prince von Bülow,* translated by F. A. Voigt, 4 vols. (Boston: Little, Brown & Co., 1931).

Davis, Oscar King. *Released for Publication: Some Inside Political History of Theodore Roosevelt and His Times, 1898–1918* (Boston: Houghton Mifflin Co., 1925).

Einstein, Lewis. *A Diplomat Looks Back,* Lawrence E. Gelfand (ed.) (New Haven: Yale University Press, 1968).

Gleichen, Major-General Lord Edward. *A Guardsman's Memoirs* (London: W. Blackwood & Sons, Ltd., 1932).

Grey of Fallodon, Viscount (Edward). *Twenty-five Years, 1892–1916,* 2 vols. (New York: Frederick A. Stokes Co., 1925).

Griscom, Lloyd C. *Diplomatically Speaking* (Boston: Little, Brown & Co., 1940).

Hardinge, Lord. *Old Diplomacy: The Reminiscences of Lord Hardinge of Penshurst* (London: J. Murray, 1947).

Howard, Esmé William. *Theatre of Life,* 2 vols. (London: Hodder & Stoughton, Ltd., 1936).

Jusserand, Jean Jules. *What Me Befell: The Reminiscences of J. J. Jusserand* (Boston and New York: Houghton Mifflin Co., 1933).

Korostovetz, J. J. *Pre-War Diplomacy: The Russo-Japanese Problem, Treaty Signed at Portsmouth, U. S. A., Diary of J. J. Korostovetz* (London: British Periodicals Ltd., 1920).

Leary, John J., Jr. *Talks with T. R.* (Boston and New York: Houghton Mifflin Co., 1920).

Paléologue, Maurice. *Three Critical Years (1904–05–06)* (New York: Robert Speller & Sons, 1957).

Phillips, William. *Ventures in Diplomacy* (Boston: Beacon Press, 1952).

Roosevelt, Theodore. *Theodore Roosevelt: An Autobiography* (New York: Charles Scribner's Sons, 1929).

Strachey, John St. Loe. *Adventure of Living: A Subjective Autobiography, 1860–1922* (New York and London: G. P. Putnam's Sons, 1922).

Wilson, Francis M. Huntington. *Memoirs of An Ex-Diplomat* (Boston: Bruce Humphries, Inc., 1945).

Witte, Serge. *The Memoirs of Count Witte,* translated and edited by Abraham Yarmolinsky (Garden City, N. Y.: Doubleday, Page & Co., 1921).

IV. BIOGRAPHIES

Blum, John Morton. *The Republican Roosevelt* (Cambridge, Mass.: Harvard University Press, 1954).

Cortissoz, Royal. *The Life of Whitelaw Reid,* 2 vols. (New York: Charles Scribner's Sons, 1921).

Croly, Herbert. *Willard Straight* (New York: The Macmillan Co., 1924).

Dennett, Tyler. *John Hay: From Poetry to Politics* (New York: Dodd, Mead & Co., 1933).

Dugdale, Blanche Elizabeth Campbell. *Arthur James Balfour, First Earl of Balfour,* 2 vols. (New York: G. P. Putnam's Sons, 1937).

Fisher, H. A. L. *James Bryce (Viscount Bryce of Dechmont, O. M.),* 2 vols. (New York: The Macmillan Co., 1927).

Garraty, John A. *Henry Cabot Lodge* (New York: A. A. Knopf, 1953).

Harbaugh, William Henry. *Power and Responsibility: The Life and Times of Theodore Roosevelt* (New York: Farrar, Straus & Cudahy, 1961).

Howe, M. A. De Wolfe. *George von Lengerke Meyer, His Life and Public Services* (New York: Dodd, Mead & Co., 1920).

Jessup, Philip C. *Elihu Root,* 2 vols. (New York: Dodd, Mead & Co., 1938).

Lee, Sir Sidney. *Edward VII, A Biography,* 2 vols. (New York: The Macmillan Co., 1925–1927).

Leopold, Richard W. *Elihu Root and the Conservative Tradition* (Boston: Little, Brown & Co., 1954).

Nevins, Allan. *Henry White: Thirty Years of American Diplomacy* (New York: Harper & Bros., 1930).

Newton, Lord (Thomas). *Lord Lansdowne, A Biography* (London: Macmillan & Co., 1929).

Nicolson, Sir Harold. *Portrait of a Diplomatist; Sir Arthur Nicolson, Bart., First Lord Carnook: A Study in the Old Diplomacy* (Boston and New York: Houghton Mifflin Co., 1930).

Porter, Charles W. *The Career of Théophile Delcassé* (Philadelphia: University of Pennsylvania Press, 1936).

Pringle, Henry F. *Theodore Roosevelt* (New York: Harcourt, Brace & Co., 1931).

Rich, Norman R. *Friedrich von Holstein,* 2 vols. (Cambridge, England: Cambridge University Press, 1965).

Strachey, Amy Simpson. *St. Loe Strachey: His Life and His Paper* (London: Victor Gollancz, 1930).

Sykes, Sir Percey M. *The Right Honourable Sir Mortimer Durand* (London: Cassell & Co., Ltd., 1926).

Trevelyan, George M. *Grey of Fallodon: The Life and Letters of Sir Edward Grey, afterwards Viscount Grey of Fallodon* (Boston and New York: Houghton Mifflin Co., 1937).

Varg, Paul A. *Open Door Diplomat: The Life of W. W. Rockhill* (Urbana, Ill.: University of Illinois Press, 1952).

Young, Kenneth. *Arthur James Balfour: The Happy Life of the Politician, Prime Minister, Statesman, and Philosopher, 1848–1930* (London: G. Bell & Sons, 1963).

V. SPECIAL STUDIES

Anderson, Eugene N. *The First Moroccan Crisis, 1904–1906* (Chicago: University of Chicago Press, 1930).

Beale, Howard K. *Theodore Roosevelt and the Rise of America to World Power* (Baltimore: Johns Hopkins Press, 1956).

Bourne, Kenneth. *Britain and the Balance of Power in North America, 1815–1908* (Berkeley and Los Angeles: University of California Press, 1967).

Campbell, Alexander E. *Great Britain and the United States, 1895–1903* (London: Longmans, 1960).

Campbell, Charles S. *Anglo-American Understanding, 1898–1903* (Baltimore: Johns Hopkins Press, 1957).

Clyde, Paul H. *International Rivalries in Manchuria, 1689–1922*, 2nd ed. (Columbus: The Ohio State University Press, 1928).

Dennis, Alfred L. P. *Adventures in American Diplomacy, 1896–1906* (New York: E. P. Dutton & Co., 1928).

Esthus, Raymond A. *Theodore Roosevelt and Japan* (Seattle: University of Washington Press, 1966).

Fay, Sidney B. *The Origins of the World War*, 2nd ed., 2 vols. in 1 (New York: The Macmillan Co., 1941).

Gelber, Lionel Morris. *The Rise of Anglo-American Friendship: A Study in World Politics, 1898–1906*, 2nd printing (Hamden, Connecticut: Archon Books, 1966).

Graebner, Norman A. *An Uncertain Tradition: American Secretaries of State in the Twentieth Century* (New York: McGraw-Hill, 1961).

Hale, Oron J. *Publicity and Diplomacy, with Special Reference to England and Germany, 1890–1914* (New York and London: D. Appleton-Century Inc., 1940).

Marder, Arthur J. *The Anatomy of British Sea Power; A History of British Naval Policy in the Pre-dreadnought Era, 1880–1905* (New York: A. A. Knopf, 1940).

Marder, Arthur J. *From the Dreadnought to Scapa Flow; the Royal Navy in the Fisher Era, 1904–1919*, Vol. I (London and New York: Oxford University Press, 1961).

Monger, George. *The End of Isolation: British Foreign Policy, 1900–1907* (London and New York: Thomas Nelson & Sons, 1963).

155

Mowry, George E. *The Era of Theodore Roosevelt, 1900–1912* (New York: Harper & Bros., 1958).

Neu, Charles E. *An Uncertain Friendship: Theodore Roosevelt and Japan, 1906–1909* (Cambridge: Harvard University Press, 1967).

Nish, Ian H. *The Anglo-Japanese Alliance: The Diplomacy of Two Island Empires, 1894–1907* (London: Athlone Press, 1966).

Perkins, Bradford. *The Great Rapproachement: England and the United States, 1895–1914* (New York: Atheneum, 1968).

Schieber, Clara Eve. *The Transformation of American Sentiment Toward Germany, 1870–1914* (Boston and New York: The Cornhill Publishing Co., 1923).

Takeuchi, Tatsuji. *War and Diplomacy in the Japanese Empire* (Garden City, N. Y.: Doubleday, Doran & Co., 1935).

Trani, Eugene P. *The Treaty of Portsmouth: An Adventure in American Diplomacy* (Lexington, Ky.: University of Kentucky Press, 1969).

Vevier, Charles. *The United States and China, 1906–1913: A Study of Finance and Diplomacy* (New Brunswick, N. J.: Rutgers University Press, 1955).

White, John A. *The Diplomacy of the Russo-Japanese War* (Princeton, N. J.: Princeton University Press, 1964).

Woodward, E. Llewellyn. *Great Britain and the German Navy* (Oxford: The Clarendon Press, 1935).

Vagts, Alfred. *Deutschland und die Vereinigten Staaten in der Weltpolitik,* 2 vols. (New York: The Macmillan Co., 1935).

Zabriskie, Edward H. *American-Russian Rivalry in the Far East, 1895–1914* (Philadelphia: University of Pennsylvania Press, 1946).

VI. ARTICLES

Askew, William C., and J. Fred Rippy, "The United States and Europe's Strife, 1908–1913," *Journal of Politics,* IV (1942), pp. 68–79.

Blake, Nelson M. "Ambassadors at the Court of Theodore Roosevelt," *Mississippi Valley Historical Review,* XLII (1955–1956), pp. 179–206.

Einstein, Lewis. "The United States and Anglo-German Rivalry," *National Review,* LX (1913), pp. 736–750.

Esthus, Raymond A. "The Changing Concept of the Open Door, 1899–1910," *Mississippi Valley Historical Review,* XLVI (1959–1960), pp. 435–454.

Esthus, Raymond A. "The Taft–Katsura Agreement — Reality or Myth," *Journal of Modern History,* XXXI (1959), pp. 46–51.

Gordon, D. C. "Roosevelt's 'Smart Yankee Trick,'" *Pacific Historical Review,* XXX (1961), pp. 351–358.

Hall, Luella J. "The Abortive German-American-Chinese Entente of 1907–08," *Journal of Modern History, I* (1929), pp. 219–235.

Hall, Luella J. "A Partnership in Peacemaking: Theodore Roosevelt and Wilhelm II," *Pacific Historical Review, XIII* (1944), pp. 390–411.

Livermore, Seward W. "The American Navy as a Factor in World Politics, 1903–1913," *American Historical Review, LXIII* (1957–1958), pp. 863–879.

Livermore, Seward W. "Theodore Roosevelt, the American Navy, and the Venezuelan Crisis," *American Historical Review, LI* (1945–1946), pp. 452–471.

Taylor, A. J. P. "The Conference at Algeciras," in *From Napoleon to Lenin* (New York: Harper and Row, 1966), Chapter xvii.

Index

Rich, Norman, 109n
Rockhill, William W., 22–23, 138, 141, 144
Roosevelt, Franklin D., 1, 23
Roosevelt, Mrs. Theodore, 11, 14, 131
Roosevelt, Theodore
  and isolationism, 2–3, 70, 83–84
  relations with State Department officials, 5–10
  diplomatic contacts with Britain, 10–13, 24
  friendship with Jusserand, 13–17, 24
  friendship with Sternburg, 15–16, 18–19, 23–24
  diplomatic contacts with Russia, 19–21
  diplomatic contacts with Japan and China, 21–23
  and Russian occupation of Manchuria, 25–27
  and Russo-Japanese War, 28–32, 41–43, 45–46, 50, 52–53
  and Portsmouth Peace Conference, 32–37, 62–63
  attitude toward Germany, 38–40, 42, 44, 46, 47–48, 50–51, 53–54, 59, 60–61, 62, 84–85, 112, 149–150
  attitude toward Britain, 38–40, 44, 45–46, 47–48, 62, 65, 112, 131–132
  attitude toward William II, 38, 55–56, 59, 61, 63, 80, 109–110, 112–113, 114, 126–127, 128–129, 130–131
  and Venezuelan crisis, 40–41
  and Moroccan crisis, 42, 57–59, 66–67, 70–87, 93–94
  on Anglo-German naval rivalry, 47–48, 60–61, 115–117, 128, 134–135, 149–150
  visit of Spring Rice, 48–52
  and Edward VII, 51, 54–56, 63, 114–115, 132
  Anglo-Japanese Alliance, 63–65
  Taft-Katsura conversation, 64
  and Algeciras Conference, 90–92, 95n, 97–111
  and Second Hague Conference, 115–117

  and Japanese-American crises, 118–123, 148–149
  and proposed German-Chinese-American Alliance, 123–127
  and Hale interview, 126–130
  on Daily Telegraph interview, 128–129
  and Root-Takahira exchange of notes, 131, 144–146
  attitude toward Japanese position in Manchuria, 137–139, 141, 144–147
Roosevelt, Theodore, Jr., 28
Root, Elihu
  and Roosevelt, 5, 6–9
  role as Secretary of State, 8–9
  and Algeciras Conference, 8, 85, 91, 92, 95, 96, 97, 100–101, 103, 106, 108, 109
  and South Manchuria, 8, 137, 141–149
  on F. M. Huntington Wilson, 10
  and Durand, 13
  and Aoki, 22
  and Rockhill, 23
  and Second Hague Conference, 117
  and Anglo-American relations, 118
  Root-Takahira exchange of notes, 127, 131, 139, 144–146
  and Washington Conference of 1921–1922, 147–148
Rosen, Baron Roman, 30
Rouvier, Maurice, 76, 77, 78, 80, 83–84
Russia
  Russo-Japanese War, 2, 3, 27–32, 36, 46–47, 77
  Roosevelt's diplomatic contacts with, 19–21
  occupation of Manchuria, 25–27
  prewar negotiations with Japan, 26–27
  Portsmouth Peace Conference, 30–35
  possible alliance with Germany, 46–47
  and Algeciras Conference, 93
  Anglo-Russian entente, 114, 123
  Russo-Japanese entente, 123, 136, 138
  postwar policy in Manchuria, 136, 137, 142–144, 147